D0287644

THE PROBLEM OF SUFFERING
IN THE OLD TESTAMENT

A

THE PROBLEM OF SUFFERING
IN THE OLD TESTAMENT

BY

ARTHUR S. PEAKE, M.A.

Professor of Biblical Exegesis in the University of Manchester
Tutor in the Primitive Methodist College, and Lecturer in Lancashire
Independent College ; Sometime Fellow of Merton College
and Lecturer in Mansfield College, Oxford

Dieu, c'est le mot de l'énigme du monde :
Jésus-Christ, c'est le mot de l'énigme de Dieu.

RAYMOND BRUCKER

THE EPWORTH PRESS

(EDGAR C. BARTON)

25-35 City Road, London, E.C.1

First published 1904
This edition 1947

Made and Printed in Great Britain
by A. W. Duncan & Co. Ltd., Liverpool

Preface

WHEN I accepted the invitation to deliver the Hartley Lecture, I selected 'The Problem of Suffering in the Old Testament' as my subject, for reasons that will be plain to all who read the last chapter of this book. I am only one of many, for whom the problem of pain constitutes the most powerful objection to a Theism, adequate to our deepest needs. I am well aware that to some I shall seem to drug my doubt with the anodyne of the Gospel. Yet I shall be more than content if by my witness-bearing I help some souls, to whom the world's misery is a nightmare, to escape beyond it into untroubled peace.

I am only too conscious how far the book is from what I had wished to make it. A serious operation in November 1902 has dislocated all my work, and the addition of new claims and duties to an already crowded life has made some of my plans impracticable. I had intended to give a full summary of the discussions in Germany and elsewhere, that for the last thirteen years have raged about the figure of the Servant of Yahweh; to compile a critical bibliography; to complete my commentary on Job; to deal much more thoroughly with the subjects treated in the last chapter. But half the book had to be written in a month, with College and review work, committees and meetings, absorbing most of my time and strength. I trust, however, that I have said the essential things, and though I might have read more, had leisure been granted me, I do not think the views I have formed would have undergone any substantial modification.

Perhaps I owe some explanation to my old pupils of the change in my views with reference to the Servant of Yahweh. I have never wavered in my belief that the Servant should be identified with Israel, and have not suffered myself to be fascinated by Duhm's powerful plea for an individual identification ; but in common with several scholars, the view that the Servant is the historical Israel seemed to me exposed to fatal objections, so I gave my adhesion to the theory that the Servant is the ideal Israel, as it has been expounded, among others, especially by Professor Skinner in his valuable commentary on Isaiah 40–66 in the *Cambridge Bible*—but I was all the while acutely conscious of its difficulties, and held it only for want of a better. The most natural view seemed to be that the historical Israel was intended throughout, and I was fully prepared to move to this more consistent position, if the objections to it could be taken out of the way. It is to Giesebrecht above all that I owe the removal of these difficulties, though in this connexion I have also to mention Budde and Marti.

The critical problems of Habakkuk cost me a great deal of trouble, which led to an unexpected result. I have for several years hoped that a solution might be reached, if not in the form proposed by Budde, at any rate along his lines. But repeated study has driven me to the conclusion that neither Budde's solution, nor those of G. A. Smith, Peiser, or Betteridge are really tenable, and I had perforce to accept, with Wellhausen and Nowack, the view first propounded by Giesbrecht. Not a little to my surprise I have also had to desert the usual view of the date, and place the prophecy in the exile. I much regret that

the second part of Marti's commentary on the Minor
Prophets has not yet been published, so that I have
not been able to avail myself of his discussion of this
and some other dark problems of the prophetic
literature.

Many may be astonished that I should have thought
it necessary to include a summary of the proofs that
Isaiah 40–66 is not the work of the prophet
Isaiah. I need hardly explain that this was due to
no feeling that the question was any longer in dispute.
But we need to remind ourselves how slowly the most
certain results make their way, and I anticipate that
I may have many readers to whom the tritest common-
places of criticism will come with freshness. It is
also striking that those who get hold of results, often
get hold of them so imperfectly, so that we still hear
people speaking of ' two Isaiahs', unaware that if
the book is not a unity, it must be highly complex
in its structure. I have referred very little to literature
earlier than 1892, when the publication of Duhm's
Commentary on Isaiah opened a new era in the
criticism and interpretation of the book.

I regret that it has been necessary to add so many
footnotes ; but for the most part they touch questions
of textual criticism, and since the text seemed so
often to need emendation, a detailed statement of
reasons was necessary. Those who are alive to the
difficulties of the received text will not, I believe,
charge me with wanton criticism. While we ought
to be done with superstitious illusions as to the
soundness of the Massoretic text, the textual critic
always needs to be on his guard against subjectivity,
arbitrariness, and violence. And lest anyone should
imagine that emendations are put forward as any-

thing more than tentative suggestions as to what the
author may have written, it may be said explicitly
that though in many cases it may be tolerably plain
that the text is corrupt, it is only a few corrections
that are fairly certain, while all degrees of probability,
or plausibility, attach to the rest.

My debt to other scholars will be evident to those
who are familiar with the subject. But I wish especially
to acknowledge the kindness of two friends. My
colleague, Professor Hope W. Hogg, Professor of
Semitic Languages and Literature in the University
of Manchester, has made time, amid a pressure of other
work, that doubles my obligation, to read my proofs.
He is in no way responsible for what I have written,
but it has reassured me to have my work read by
so competent and accurate a scholar.   My friend,
Miss Mabel Frith, has read my proofs and made
suggestions which I have been glad to adopt.   I have
to thank her not only for this and for the keen interest
she has taken in the book, but for the quotation
from Raymond Brucker, that I have placed on the
title page.

ARTHUR S. PEAKE

Manchester
   28th May 1904

Contents

CHAPTER THREE

THE SERVANT OF YAHWEH

Chapter Four

A CENTURY OF DISILLUSION

Chapter Five

THE PROBLEM IN JOB

CHAPTER SIX

SONGS IN THE NIGHT

CHAPTER SEVEN

THE APOCALYPTIST AND THE PESSIMIST

CHAPTER ONE

The Rise of the Problem

IT was not till a comparatively late period in the history of Israel that the problem of suffering engaged the attention of her thinkers. The ancient Hebrews, like kindred peoples, looked on their disasters as a token of the Divine anger. This anger might be kindled by national sin, or it might be the mysterious expression of a fitful mood. The latter view could not, of course, be seriously entertained alongside of a worthier conception of God, so we find the Biblical writers for the most part tracing the wrath of God to the disobedience of His people. The historians tell us how the Israelites forsook Yahweh and were sold to other nations, till they returned to their God, and He gave them their desire upon their enemies. To this conviction of the close connexion between sin and suffering, the prophets again and again appealed. Thus Isaiah, speaking to his countrymen, when Judah had been scourged by Sennacherib, till from head to foot it was one festering sore, chides the infatuation which blinds them to the truth and sternly utters Yahweh's ultimatum : ' Come now, and let us reason together, saith Yahweh : if your sins are as scarlet, shall they be as white as snow? if they be red like crimson, shall they be as wool ? If ye be willing and obedient, ye shall eat the good of the land : but if ye refuse and rebel, ye shall be devoured with the sword : for the mouth of Yahweh hath spoken it.'

I

Under Manasseh, religion and morality went from
bad to worse. The prophetic party was bitterly
persecuted, old abuses were revived, and strange
forms of worship were introduced. His reign seemed
to a later generation the adequate cause for the
misery soon to fall on Judah. With the accession
of Josiah in 639 B.C. new hope dawned for the higher
religion of Israel. The prophets, who had been
driven to work underground, now found the times
propitious, and laboured with such success that when
in 621 B.C. the Deuteronomic Law was discovered,
the seed fell on a soil not wholly uncongenial. Terror-
struck at its threats against disobedience, Josiah
carried through a drastic reformation. Since the
Law had set before the people a blessing or a curse,
conditional on obedience or disobedience to its com-
mands, the prompt and whole-hearted execution of
the reforms it demanded seemed to promise that the
nation's long warfare had drawn to its close. Judah
was at last a righteous people, then it must be
prosperous, for law and prophets had combined to
declare that it should be well with the righteous.

But this bright illusion was soon shattered by a
series of disasters. Josiah, unwilling to exchange
his almost unfettered freedom, under the suzerainty
of a decadent Assyria, for servitude to Pharaoh-
necoh, the Egyptian king, fought the latter at
Megiddo[a] and was killed on the field (608 B.C.). And
now the unhappy country sank more and more deeply
in misfortune. Jehoahaz was deposed after a three-

[a] So the present Hebrew text. Possibly it was farther south, in
Josiah's own territory. Herodotus (ii. 159) speaks of a defeat of the
Syrians at Magdolos. If he is referring to the same event, the name
meant would be Migdal, perhaps the Migdal-gad mentioned in Joshua
15³⁷. (See H. P. Smith's *Old Testament History*, pp 279, 280).

months' reign and taken to die as a captive in Egypt
He was succeeded by his elder brother Jehoiakim.
The Assyrian empire fell about 607 B.C., and in
605 B.C. Babylon conquered Egypt at Carchemish,
and entered on the period of its supremacy.
Jehoiakim became the vassal of Nebuchadnezzar,
and some years later rebelled.[b] He died before punishment fell on Judah, and it was reserved for his son
Jehoiachin to be carried captive to Babylon with the
flower of the nation in 597 B.C. Nebuchadnezzar
placed a brother of Jehoiakim on the throne, and
gave him the name Zedekiah. The new monarch was
weak rather than ill-disposed, and he is less to be
blamed for the reckless violation of his solemn oath
of loyalty than those who forced his hand. Un-
taught by experience and in defiance of Jeremiah's
warning, the turbulent nation, trusting, such was
its madness, in the promises of Egypt, threw off
the Babylonian yoke. This time there was no
reprieve, and the blow already steadfastly foretold
by Jeremiah for more than thirty years, fell in 586
B.C. Jerusalem and the temple were destroyed, and
the nation went into exile in Babylon.

It is generally believed that, before the last act of
this tragedy was played, a voice had already been
raised in pain and perplexity. Unhappily the
critical and historical difficulties of the Book of
Habakkuk are so serious that we cannot be at all
sure what the conditions were that created his
problem. Numerous solutions have been proposed,
each of them with its own attractions, each exposed
to grave objections.[c] The following conclusions

---

[b] The chronology is difficult. The ' three years ' of our present
Hebrew text (2 Kings 24[1]) seems too short.

[c] See Appendix A : ' Recent Criticism of Habakkuk' p. 133.

seem to the present writer to be probable. (*a*) The subject of the complaint in 1^{2-4} is the same as in 1^{12-17}, in both passages the problem rises from the oppression of righteous Judah by a heathen tyrant. (*b*) Since in these two passages the rule of the tyrant has been long established, 1^{5-11} cannot spring out of the same situation, unless in $1^{2-4,\ 12-17}$ another heathen power than the Chaldeans is intended. (*c*) Every form of the theory that the Chaldeans are raised up as instruments of judgement on another heathen power, is beset by difficulties of too serious a character to permit us to accept it. (*d*) The only alternative that remains is to regard 1^{5-11} as an older oracle, which is out of place in the present prophecy. (*e*) After 1^{5-11} has been eliminated, substantially the whole of the first two chapters is the composition of Habakkuk, and probably dates from the Exile. If, however, the usual view that the prophet wrote before the destruction of Jerusalem be correct, more of 2^{9-20} might plausibly be assigned to a later writer. (*f*) The third chapter is a post-exilic Psalm, which owes its present position to the title it bore in the collection of Psalms from which it was taken.

Although I prefer to regard the prophecy as exilic, yet in deference to the general opinion of scholars, I will speak of it at this point. It makes comparatively little difference to our estimate. If Habakkuk saw his vision in the gloomy period before the fall of Jerusalem, his problem arises because he feels so keenly the strange contrast between the fair promise of the happiness that should follow on reform, and the dark fulfilment now that reform has come. If it was during the Exile, then the destruction of the Jewish State and the captivity are responsible for much of the prophet's perplexity, and the Reformation falls into the background. But though in view of the uncertainties we cannot state problem or solution with precision, yet they may be stated with sufficient accuracy for our purpose. Speaking generally, his problem rises out of the oppression of the righteous, and the prosperity of the violent oppressor, while the answer he receives is that retribution is certainly coming, and the righteous shall live by his firm fidelity to Yahweh. He begins with a complaint of Yahweh's apparent indifference. Strange that he should cry and find Yahweh deaf so long ! for if he feels it intolerable to look on these scenes of outrage, how can Yahweh endure them, whose eyes are too pure to behold evil ? Yet the treacherous nation still pursues its course of immoral conquest. Like a fisherman, skilled in his craft, the tyrant sweeps the nations into his net,[d] and annexes them to his bloated empire. In 2^{5-20} other traits are added to the portrait : his insatiable greed, his vain ambition to lift himself beyond the reach of evil,[e] his savage gloating over the shame and agony of his victims. Is then his career of evil to go on unchecked, ' shall he not spare to slay the nations continually ' ?

As he broods over his problem, the prophetic ecstasy begins to fall upon him. In spirit he climbs the watch-tower,[f] whence he may search the secrets of heaven, and see the forces that shape the destinies of earth. The response he wins from God seems at

[d] For Budde's inference from the angling metaphor see Appendix A, p. 133.
[e] This reminds us of the story of the tower of Babel (Genesis 11^{1-9}).
[f] cf. Isaiah 21^{6-9}.

first to be meagre, and the answer one that might
have been divined from the facts already before him.
He is bidden wait in confidence for the fulfilment of
the vision, which will surely come in spite of delay.
The soul of the oppressor is puffed up, it is not
upright in him, but the just shall live by his faithfulness. If the heathen tyrant was what he had
been described to be, and if God who ruled the
universe was of too pure eyes to behold evil, the
collision of these facts could have but one issue. In
a world ruled by such a God, the triumph of wickedness was an anomaly, and anomalies cannot be
permanent in the moral order. It was not merely
that the conqueror's cruelty and violence filled
the prophet's soul with indignation, but his pride
was ominous of ruin. In his denunciation of the
former, the prophet stands in the succession of
Amos, who uttered Yahweh's sentence on the heathen
for outrages on our common humanity, and of Nahum
with his passionate execration of Nineveh and
exultation over her downfall. The feeling that
pride went before destruction was widespread in
antiquity. Men, to whom the jealousy of the gods
was a real and ever present peril, were not tempted
to flaunt their happiness in the face of heaven. To
walk softly and humbly was their safety ; pride
was an uncanny temper, that would soon draw the
lightning from the clouds. The thought that
because Yahweh is high and lifted up, there is to be
a Day of Yahweh, when all that is high and lifted
up on earth shall be abased, is very prominent in
Isaiah. But he has transformed the vindictive
jealousy of the gods into a lofty doctrine in harmony
with his conception of Yahweh not simply as

the exalted, but as the holy God. Habakkuk stands in the line of this thought and finds in the pride of the oppressor the presage of his downfall. He deifies his own strength and skill as the givers of success, just as Assyria had done according to Isaiah (10⁵⁻¹⁵). The latter prophet had spoken of Assyria as the rod of Yahweh's anger, with which He smote the nations, but which, when it had served its purpose, would be snapped asunder for its insolence, and cast away. This combination does not occur in Habakkuk if we are right in rejecting the common but very difficult view that the Chaldeans were raised up to be the instruments of Yahweh's vengeance on the sinners of Judah, and were then for their arrogance to be destroyed.

The prophet's mind is fixed on the certainty of the tyrant's overthrow, even though delay may seem to justify despair. Retribution lay in the nature of things. His empire was based on brutality, so he should perish in the blood that he had spilt. His exploits filled him with an impious arrogance, so Heaven must crush him and vindicate its outraged majesty. In the methods of swelling his empire, and the temper with which success inspired him, lurked the secret of his ruin. All this is a very impressive moral lesson that does not quickly grow out of date, but it adds nothing essentially new. The prosperity of the wicked is not explained, we are simply told that it cannot last.

Similarly, no explanation is given of the sufferings of the righteous, although the prophet demands one, and expects to receive it on his watchtower. What is given him is an assurance that they will soon be ended, and that by his fidelity the righteous shall save his life. The righteous one is Judah.⁵ It is true that in this estimate of the nation's character the prophet is sharply divided from his predecessors. This is usually explained by the fact that in the meantime the Deuteronomic Reformation had taken place. Still, on any theory which places the prophecy before the fall of Jerusalem there is difficulty. If it is the Chaldean oppression which vexes the prophet's soul, that did not begin till the reign of Jehoiakim had lasted for some years, and under that worthless monarch the Reformation had been undone, so that Judah could seem righteous only to a very optimistic gaze. If Budde is right in identifying the oppressor with Assyria, and fixing the date about 615 B.C., then it is true that Josiah was on the throne and the Reformation policy was still in force. Judah was a righteous people, externally, at any rate ; but its condition was prosperous. Assyria was decrepit, its rule altogether relaxed ; why should the prophet complain of its career of unchecked conquest, or why cry out so bitterly of his country's suffering ? The difficulty presents itself in this way. Habakkuk's problem is the prosperity of the wicked and the suffering of the righteous nation ; but, in his time, on the usual view of his date, when the nation was

⁵ The singular suggests to a modern reader that the individual is intended, every righteous one shall live by his fidelity, all the more so as the use of the passage in Hebrews, and especially in Paul's famous watchword, so far removed from the thought of the prophet, ' But he that is righteous by faith shall live ' (i.e. he shall live who is justified by faith), concentrates attention on the individual. It is, of course, possible that the reference here is individual. But it is not likely. The singular in the former part of the verse refers to the oppressing nation, and so in 1¹⁰⁻¹⁷,2⁵⁻²⁰. This makes it probable that the just is righteous Judah. On Peiser's view of the prophecy, it would apparently be the prophet himself.

righteous, it was for the most part prosperous, and during its period of wickedness its fortunes went from bad to worse.

Moreover, the question might be raised, whether at any point in this period, even the best, Judah could be described as really righteous. Jeremiah's judgement seems to have been throughout unfavourable. The reformation had not gone below the surface, there had been no essential change in the situation, from Jeremiah's point of view the problem why righteous Judah suffered did not exist. Now if they were contemporaries, we cannot deny that Jeremiah saw more deeply than Habakkuk, and was not betrayed by glittering illusions into unconsciousness of the rottenness at the nation's heart. But this need not blind us to the merits of Habakkuk. There was room for the recognition of a relative righteousness in Judah, as contrasted with the sin of the heathen, and in this he does not stand alone. Nahum is distinguished from his predecessors by his omission of all reference to the sin of his country, and by the concentration of his wrath on Assyria. And especially of the Second Isaiah is it true that while he insists on its sin, he yet regards Israel as righteous in comparison with the heathen. The difficulty is materially lightened if we place Habakkuk in the Exile. In any case he is not the mere victim of a false optimism in his estimate of Judah ; there was a problem, though all he could do in face of it was to counsel patience, and no hint of a solution was revealed to him.

While Jeremiah felt upon him no pressure of mystery in the sad fate of Judah, lacerated though

he was in his tenderest feelings by it, yet his own lot
may well have led him to ponder on the dark riddle
of God's ways. For more than thirty years he
watched his country move blindly to its doom,
incredulous of his warnings and intolerant of his
appeals. Secure in the possession of the Temple, and
resting on Isaiah's once splendidly vindicated, but
now antiquated, doctrine of the indestructibility of
Zion, the Jews mocked the message of their Cassandra,
and shot the rapids into unlooked-for ruin. Through
all this period the lot of this greatest of the prophets
was harder than we can well imagine. Filled with
a passionate love for his country, how could he be
other than broken-hearted, as he sat long years by
the death-bed of his nation, well knowing that there
was no longer room for hope ? ' The harvest is
past, the summer is ended, and we are not saved.
. . Oh that my head were waters, and mine eyes
a fountain of tears, that I might weep day and
night for the slain of the daughter of my people.'
But there was not wanting to the bitterness of his
trouble the conviction that all its woes were the fruit
of its own ill-doing. And now to the anguish for
his people's suffering, and the deeper anguish for its
sin, there was added that which sprang from the
tragedy of his own career. He was forced, in loyalty
to his vocation, to set himself against the cherished
illusions of his countrymen, in vain attempt to stem
the torrent, which bore them like a mill race to their
doom. He denounces their sins, idolatry, violence,
oppression, fraud, theft, and murder, their trust in
the temple of Yahweh as a fetish assuring their
safety, unmindful of the fate that had blotted out
Shiloh, their schemes of rebellion, their desperate

warfare against inexorable facts. He bids the exiles
in Babylon reconcile themselves to captivity, he
warns the remnant in Jerusalem to submit while
there is yet time. Thus in spite of his pure and lofty
patriotism he seemed a faint-hearted traitor, who
stole the people's courage by his gloomy fore-
bodings. Again and again he risked death at the
hands of his infuriated countrymen. Had he been
of that temperament which seeks its joy in conflict
and rebukes transgression with a stern delight,
he had been a happier man. But sensitive and
high-strung, with unplumbed depths of tenderness and yearning affection, his life of contention
was an intolerable burden. He pines for a lodge in
the wilderness away from the strife of tongues,
away from the treachery and deceit that have
poisoned all their relations of life. He curses the day
of his birth to see labour and sorrow. He laments
that his pain is perpetual, and his wound refuses to be
healed. He has become a laughing-stock to the
people, and his message meets always with derision.
Terror is all about him, dark and sinister schemes are
plotted for his destruction. Fain would he yield to
the forces which would drive him from his post, fain
abandon the unequal struggle into which he has
suffered Yahweh to entice him. Yet Yahweh will
not let him escape, but bends His reluctant servant to
His will by the intolerable compulsion of His word.
' And if I say, I will not make mention of Him, nor
speak any more in His name, then there is in mine
heart as it were a burning fire shut up in my bones
and I am weary with forbearing, and I cannot
contain.' A lonely man, forbidden the sweet solace
of wife and children, mocked and misunderstood by

those whom he longed to save, when the sharp agony broke down its self-restraint and forced him out of himself, to whom could he turn for sympathy but to God ? In a strange tumult his soul goes out to God, mingling bitter reproach for the pain and scorn He has made him suffer, with prayers for vengeance on his enemies, exultation at God's presence with him, and gladness in the fellowship which he enjoys with God. Yet his pleadings do not make God swerve from His purpose. He gains the assurance that his enemies shall not prevail against him. But even before his birth Yahweh had chosen him to fulfil His great design.   Therefore he cannot receive discharge from his warfare. Nay, he may look to a yet severer conflict. When he pleads the incon-sistency between the righteousness of God and the prosperity of the wicked, the baffled prophet receives the reply, ' If thou hast run with the footmen and they have wearied thee, then how canst thou con-tend with horses ? and if in a land of peace thou fleest, how wilt thou do in the pride of Jordan ? '[h]   It was then, with no light on his suffering, save that it was incident to the work God had appointed for him, that Jeremiah had to set his face like a flint and go wearily forward with a task more bitter than death.

It lies beyond my scope to discuss the function of suffering as a medium of revelation. Yet at this point I may be suffered so far to transgress my limits as to indicate the part it played in transforming the conception of religion. It was this life of unceasing sorrow, this isolation and misunderstanding, that

---

[h] Duhm regards 12¹⁻⁵ as the work of a later writer. I read *bōreach* for *bōteach* with Hitzig, Cornill, and Duhm.

forced the prophet from man to God. To him He lays bare his troubles, refers his tangled perplexities, utters his keen reproaches or exulting confidence. Beyond other men he is driven into intimate fellowship with God, till it becomes a necessity of his religious life. Thus he came to understand religion as a personal relation between himself and God ; thus the individual, not the State, became the religious unit. Hence, while his greatest doctrine, that of the New Covenant, still speaks of a covenant made with the nation, yet its fulfilment on Israel's part is guaranteed by the fact that God puts His law in their inward parts, and writes it on their heart, so that for himself each individual knows Him.[i] It was

[i] In the first edition of his *Alttestamentliche Religionsgeschichte* (1893) Smend argued strongly that the New Covenant passage (Jeremiah 31^{31-4}) originated in the post-exilic period (pp. 239–41). His argument rested largely on his conclusion that Jeremiah 30–1 reflected the conditions of the post-exilic period. I think that his arguments carry conviction for considerable sections of these two chapters. But I do not think that the recognition of a large post-exilic element in them requires us to pass this judgement on the prediction of a New Covenant. I had independently reached this view of Smend's arguments a good while before I found that Giesebrecht adopts the same position in his *Commentary on Jeremiah*. I am not convinced that the prophecy of a New Covenant presupposes, as Smend argues, that the old Covenant had been already abrogated by the destruction of Jerusalem. For many years before it happened, that catastrophe had been a prophetic certainty to Jeremiah ; is it incredible that he had meditated on the future relations of Yahweh and Israel ? And if the Old Covenant had failed, what more likely than that he should anticipate a New Covenant ? The form which this should take was naturally determined largely by his own religious ideal. This, as we see from other passages, was inward rather than external, and his experience had driven him to seek his own religious satisfaction in personal fellowship with God. This, in spite of Smend's denial, is, I think, the essential meaning of the passage. I believe the doctrine of the New Covenant to be Jeremiah's, on the ground of its harmony with his teaching, of the fact that he elsewhere expresses the same thought, though less definitely, of the possibility of explaining it out of his personal experience, and its remarkable relevance to the historical situation. I may add that Marti, in his *Geschichte der israelitischen Religion*

ample reward for all his sufferings to have this great experience and to enshrine it in a doctrine in which Christ and the Apostles recognized a fit expression of Christianity.[j]

[j] 1 Corinthians 11[25], cf. Mark 14[24], Matthew 26[28]; 2 Corinthians 3[6]. The passage underlies much of the argument of the Epistle to the Hebrews.

(1897, p. 120), maintained the authenticity of the passage, similarly Cheyne in his *Jewish Religious Life after the Exile* (1898, p. 253). In the second edition of the work already mentioned (1899) Smend reaffirms his position, and says that he has not been convinced by Giesebrecht's arguments. In his article ' Covenant ' in the *Encyclopædia Biblica*, Professor Schmidt, of Cornell, treats the passage as post-exilic, and repeats this view in his very radical article on ' Jeremiah'. Duhm adopts the same position in his recent *Commentary on Jeremiah* (1901). This is the most significant fact on that side of the controversy. It is true that Duhm's treatment of the book is radical, but Duhm the critic is not the measure of Duhm the interpreter of ideas, and least of all in this case. He has a genuine enthusiasm for Jeremiah, and it is with much reluctance that he has felt himself unable to escape the force of Smend's arguments. Perhaps we might see in this a Nemesis on his general critical theory of the book.

CHAPTER TWO

Ezekiel

THE problem of suffering did not become acute till Jerusalem had fallen. Even after Jehoiachin and the best of the nation had gone into captivity in 597 B.C., the buoyant optimism of the people still scorned the solid ground of facts. The prophets fed their fantastic hopes with brilliant predictions, the offspring of a dogma estranged from ethics and out of touch with reality. In two years, so Hananiah prophesied early in Zedekiah's reign, the yoke of Babylon should be broken, and the vessels of the Lord's house, the king and the captives should return to Jerusalem (Jeremiah 28). In Babylon also the prophets fervently proclaimed the speedy end of the Exile and denounced Jeremiah for his warning that the captivity would be long (Jeremiah 29). Many in Jerusalem, indeed, entertained the strange delusion that they were far better than those who had gone to Babylon, and that while the exiles were abandoned of God, the fact that they were spared was a guarantee of Yahweh's favour. But apart from some, who despairing of Yahweh had resorted to primitive superstitions, or other forms of idolatry (Ezekiel 8), one and all, in Jerusalem and in Babylon, despising the admonitions of Jeremiah and Ezekiel, held firmly to the conviction that Jerusalem could not be destroyed.

When these glittering bubbles broke against the brutal realities of a city in flames and a nation in captivity, the problem of suffering became the burning question for the people. It was solved in various ways. Many held that the cause of their trouble was to be found in the weakness or indifference of Yahweh, and some had yielded to this feeling even before the fall of the city (Ezekiel, $8^{12,}$ 9^9). It was only to be expected that a people which spurned the teaching of Jeremiah, and had not absorbed the spiritual side of prophetic doctrine, should readily see in the national disasters the defeat of the nation's God. Or they said that Yahweh had forgotten them, or that He had forsaken His land. Some even went so far as to ascribe their misfortunes to their exclusive worship of Yahweh. In the very instructive narrative in Jeremiah 44 we read that the fugitives in Egypt met Jeremiah's rebuke of their idolatry and prophecy of extermination with a resolute refusal to abandon their ways. Rather they would continue to burn incense to the Queen of Heaven, for while they still served her they had lived in abundance and seen no evil. But since they had ceased to serve her, they tell the prophet, ' we have wanted all things, and have been consumed by the sword and the famine'. There was, indeed, much plausibility in their argument. With Josiah's Reformation there had not come the permanent good fortune that had been anticipated. Less than quarter of a century had seen the death of Josiah, the Egyptian and then the Chaldean oppression with the first captivity. In eleven years more, temple and city were a smoking ruin. And now the unhappy remnant, left behind in Judah, had fled to Egypt, dreading the vengeance of Nebuchadnezzar for Ishmael's treacherous murder of Gedaliah, the governor. From their standpoint something was to be said for the belief that the source of their misery was unfaithfulness to the Queen of Heaven. No doubt they were typical of many more in Babylon. They have no significance for later history, since they would quickly lose their racial identity and be merged with the heathen among whom they dwelt. The religious future lay with those who held fast to Yahweh.

The temper of these was one of deep discouragement, mingled with resentment against their God. Their despair found expression in the popular saying, ' Our bones are dried up, and our hope is lost ; we are clean cut off ' (Ezekiel 37^{11}). To uproot this settled conviction of the nation's extinction, Ezekiel narrates his wonderful vision of the valley of dry bones. In the spirit he is taken to Jerusalem, and there he sees the valley filled with a vast number of bones. And as he is led to walk tenderly about them, not crushing them with his feet, he scans them more closely and sees that they are very dry. The flesh has rotted away or birds and beasts have picked the skeletons clean, and then the skeletons have fallen to pieces, and all that is left is a mass of isolated bones. And these have lost all sap of vitality, so that had it not been Yahweh who put it, the question ' Son of man, can these dry bones live ? ' would have seemed a mere mockery. The prophet can only answer reverently : ' O Lord Yahweh, Thou knowest.' Then he is bidden prophesy over the bones. The

prophetic word has within it an inherent energy,
which works on to its own fulfilment (Isaiah 55¹¹).
So, as he prophesies over them, bone seeks its mate
till skeletons are complete, then these are clothed
with sinews, flesh, and skin. Still they are only
dead bodies, so the prophet has once more to
prophesy for the breath to come from the four winds
and breathe into the dead that they may live. And
as this is accomplished they stand on their feet an
exceeding great army.

This vision seems at first to bear only indirectly
on our subject. But it shows in a very striking way
how profound was the hopelessness of the people.
The nation was as dead as the dry bones that Ezekiel
saw bleaching in the valley. Moreover, this
metaphor of death, in the sense of national dissolution, will meet us again in a very important
connexion. It is true, however, that Ezekiel's
message that Yahweh will cause the people to come
up out of their graves has little relevance to the
problem of Israel's suffering.

But mingled with the people's despondency was
a feeling of resentment against their God ; and this
is important alike for the view of the Israelites and of
Ezekiel. It found expression in the proverb which
Jeremiah and Ezekiel tell us was current among their
contemporaries : ' The fathers have eaten sour grapes,
and the children's teeth are set on edge ' (Jeremiah
31²⁹, Ezekiel 18²).

This was a very natural explanation of their
misfortunes. It rested on the ancient belief in
solidarity, which went back to a very primitive
social condition, but which was now provoking
ethical criticism. That the sins of the fathers

were visited on the children to the third and fourth
generations was a principle expressed in the Decalogue.
We must not forget, of course, that this solidarity
did not work for evil only. While penalty passes
on to the third and fourth generations, mercy is
shown to thousands who belong to those who
love God. This feeling of unity in the life of a
people through all the stages of its history, this
sense of mutual responsibility and the punishment
of one generation for the sins of its predecessors,
was deeply wrought into the consciousness of
Israel. And the principle of retribution, expressed
in the proverb about the sour grapes, is definitely
applied by the author of the Book of Kings to the
exile of Judah. Several times he asserts that this
and the other misfortunes of Judah were due to
the sin of Manasseh (2 Kings 21[11–15], 23[26–7], 24[3–4]).
The same thought is found also in Jeremiah 15[4].
The Jews in exile did not deny the principle, they
firmly believed it to be the explanation of their
own sufferings, but they complained that it outraged their sense of justice. God was not treating
them fairly ; Manasseh sinned and they had to
suffer : ' The ways of Yahweh are not equal.' A
large section of Ezekiel's teaching was called forth
as a protest against this accusation.

This prophet, who had gone into exile with
Jehoiachin in 597 B.C., held a position of high
responsibility. When Jerusalem fell in 586
Jeremiah's life work was all but done. But Ezekiel,
whose call came to him in 592, had the task laid
upon him, not simply of delivering the message of
judgement before the final stroke fell on the ' rebellious house ', but of confronting the new conditions

and preparing for the restoration. His prophetic
career was controlled by the fundamental conception
of the glory of Yahweh, which had been stamped
into his soul by the vision which made him a prophet.
We might almost call him the Calvin of the Old
Testament. His temperament was very different
from Jeremiah's. He lacked his tenderness, his
sympathy, his deep love, his passionate longing to
be loved ; he stood in the succession of Amos, and
Isaiah, and Micah, rather than in the succession of
Hosea and Jeremiah. His severity made the word
of judgement congenial to him, while Jeremiah's keen
denunciations, like Hosea's, quiver with his pain.
Nor is there any trace in his relations with God of
that intimate communion which is so characteristic
of Jeremiah. He falls prostrate before the blinding
brightness of His glory, and knows himself to be but
a frail child of man in contrast with the all-powerful
and all-holy God. As he gazes upon Him, he is
crushed, like Isaiah, by the sense of his own un-
worthiness, and realizes the hideous uncleanness of his
people. He thinks of Yahweh as seeking in all things
His own glory, keenly resenting all encroachment on
His honour and jealously guarding His holy Name
from all that would profane it. His own problem is
therefore not to reconcile with justice the hard fate
of Israel, but to clear the fair fame of Yahweh from
the aspersions cast upon it. If he seeks to justify
the ways of God to man, it is rather that God may
be vindicated, than that man's heart may be at
peace. He never felt the pressure of the mystery
of suffering ; where Yahweh governed, to recognize
a problem was to challenge the equity of His rule
Nevertheless, the problem existed for others, if not

for himself, and so it came about that he had to
discuss it.

With remarkable courage he repudiates the earlier
conception of solidarity. It is wholly untrue to say
that the Jews are suffering for the sins of their
fathers. There is no such thing as vicarious punishment, or vicarious reward. The father cannot suffer
for the sin of the son, nor the son for the sin of his
father. It is not true that the soul that sins shall
escape, and another perish in his stead. The soul
that sins, it and no other shall die. ' The righteousness of the righteous shall be put down to his own
account, and the wickedness of the wicked to his own
account ' (18[20]). The misfortunes of the people
were therefore not, as they, in agreement with their
own historian, urged, a penalty for the sins of
Manasseh, but the just reward of their own.

This doctrine of individual responsibility created
a revolution in religious thought and life. It is easy
to criticize it, and show that the doctrine of solidarity
expressed a truth deeply rooted in experience. The
old saying is true that the sins of the fathers are
visited on the children. We are members one of
another, no man lives to himself, our character and
conduct alike are largely determined, for good or ill,
by forces in whose release we had no share. It is
not by denying patent facts that we shall vindicate
the order under which we live. Yet Ezekiel's doctrine
of individual responsibility is not on that account to
be brushed aside as illegitimate. Not only does it
express a great truth, but a truth that needed just
then to be asserted, even in an exaggerated form.
To the man, who bore on his consience the load of
a guilt not his own, the prophet spoke a liberating

word : a man has to answer only for sins he has himself committed. To those, who thought that the righteousness of the fathers availed to make good deficiencies of their own, the stern law is proclaimed that none can be saved by the good deeds of another, even of the best. There is no transfer of merit, there is, indeed, no superfluous merit to be transferred. ' Though these three men, Noah, Daniel, and Job were in it, they should deliver but their own souls by their righteousness, saith the Lord Yahweh ' (14^{14}). But the prophet carries the thought a stage farther. In the exercise of his freedom a man may change his whole course of life, the wicked may turn from his wickedness, or the righteous from his righteousness. Habit does not bind him in shackles that he cannot burst. And just as the sin or goodness of others does not involve him in any consequences, so little does the sin or goodness of his own past life. The prophet looks forward to the great impending judgement which is to fall on Israel. When this takes place the righteous will survive and the wicked be slain. The fate of each individual is determined by the accident of his condition at the moment when judgement is executed. If he has a long past of sin behind him, but has repented of his wickedness, then he shall be spared, and all his former evil life shall not be remembered against him. If on the other hand he has lived for many years in righteousness, but has been betrayed into sin, and he is in a state of sin when judgement comes, then all his long career of goodness counts for nothing in his favour, but he shall die in his sin. Thus judgement selects its victims, not in virtue of the general drift of a man's life, not in accordance with his intrinsic character, or by balancing his good against his evil deeds, but on what seems the merely arbitrary principle that all may be determined by the sheer accident of time. If judgement came a day sooner or a day later, in how many cases fate would be reversed. Yet even for this there is a relative justification. With what encouragement comes the message to the man who is fettered by habit and crushed by accumulated sins, if a voice bids him snap his chain, since he has the power, and assures him that, if he repent, not all the transgressions of a lifetime will affect his standing with God. And, once more, how salutary the warning that no man must presume on his past, so far as to be slack in his efforts, or judge that his many righteous deeds can secure him, if he lapses into sin. Thus hope comes to the despairing sinner, while the righteous is warned to relax none of his vigilance. Any moment may be the moment of destiny, life must always be strung to the highest ethical pitch. Since life and death thus hung in the balance, and this act or that might embody the fateful choice, the prophet's mission is no longer simply to the nation, but to the individual. He is responsible for uttering the warning to the righteous that he abide in his righteousness, lest he be cut off in his sin, and to the wicked that he turn from his evil way and live. He becomes a pastor, who is bound to watch for souls as one that must give account. If, when the catastrophe comes, any man be found in sin, whom the prophet had failed to warn, he must die, but God will require his blood at the prophet's hand.

It would probably be a mistake to suppose that Ezekiel learned his individualism from Jeremiah.

It is by no means certain that Jeremiah had for-
mulated his doctrine so early. There is also a wide
difference between the two doctrines. The emphasis
with Jeremiah is on personal religion, with Ezekiel
on personal responsibility. It was rather due
to the criticism passed on God's action that
Ezekiel proclaimed so uncompromising a doctrine.
Once he had said one generation cannot suffer for
the sin of another, it was only a step farther to say
that one individual cannot suffer for the sin of
another.

With all this emphasis on the correspondence
between the fate of the individual and the condition
in which he happens to be at the moment when the
storm of judgement breaks, it is remarkable to find
Ezekiel so much concerned with the past. If the
children's teeth are set on edge because they have
themselves eaten sour grapes, if they suffer for their
own sins and not for the sins of their fathers, why
does the prophet dilate at such length on the sin of
the chosen people through all its history? While
other prophets had spoken of the early purity of
Israel when Yahweh rescued her from bondage, wooed
her in the wilderness and won her for His bride,
Ezekiel sees nothing in all the stages of her career
but a series of gross acts of infidelity. With a
naked realism that strikes strangely on our finer
taste, he pictures her loathsome and insatiable
passion (Ezekiel 16, 23). All the kindness of Yahweh
had been wasted upon her. She had been idolatrous
in Egypt, and He was minded to cut her off, but in
tender regard for His holy Name, that it might not
be profaned in the sight of the heathen, He spared her
and brought her into the wilderness. But there again

she provoked Him by disobedience, and once more He lifted His hand to smite, but lest His honour should be impugned did not make a full end of her Then He brought her into the fair land of Palestine, but her change of home brought no change of disposition. She adopted the heathen sanctuaries of Canaan, and ranged abroad to Assyria and Babylon to gratify her idolatrous lust. Samaria had been destroyed, yet Jerusalem took no warning by her sister's fate, but plunged deeper in the mire of her unfaithfulness. True daughter of her Hittite mother, her history did not belie her origin. Born, only to be cast with abhorrence into the open field, she moved Yahweh to pity as He saw her lie uncared-for and weltering in her blood, and He saved her from death. Then as she grew to maidenhood, untended and forlorn, He plighted His troth to her and set His majesty upon her, so that she prospered unto royal estate, and gained renown among the nations for the perfection of her beauty. But she perverted to the basest ends the gifts wherewith His love had endowed her, and became worse even than Sodom or Samaria. Now at length the fury which has so long tormented Him will burst its restraints, and He will be quiet and rest, no longer fretted by her abominations.

This seems to represent a point of view inconsistent with the prophet's strenuous repudiation of vicarious punishment. If from his own generation is required the penalty for Israel's appalling career of wickedness, were the ways of Yahweh equal after all ? Does not the prophet's concern for Yahweh's honour lead to conflicting results ? At one time Yahweh remits the punishment, that His name may not be profaned among the heathen, but at another

time concern for His purity causes Him to react with
a drastic vengeance against its violation. In one place
Ezekiel argues that the equity of Yahweh forbids
that one generation should suffer for another,
while elsewhere he seems to represent Yahweh's
honour as vindicated by visiting on the prophet's
contemporaries the accumulated transgressions of
Israel's sinful history. We should probably solve
the difficulty by recognizing a distinction between
the nation and the individuals who compose it.
Nation and city have, so to speak, an independent
existence of their own, a continuous life, which
stretches from the days of Egyptian bondage to the
prophet's own time. He sees that Israel is about
to plunge into ruin, and the city is to be destroyed.
He stands to plead for Yahweh and make plain the
righteousness of His dealings. Thus he comes to
draw his great indictment against the nation. He
looks away wholly from the individuals who constitute
it. Yahweh and Israel, these two and the relations
between them, engage his thought. The grace of
Yahweh met by Israel's ingratitude, His honour
compromised by her infidelities, His anger once and
again restrained through pity for His holy Name,
such was the tragic story of Yahweh and of her
whom in pity He had taken for His bride. That
Israel's existence as a nation should be ended, and
that Jerusalem and its temple should be destroyed,
created a problem for those who believed in the
election of Israel and saw in the temple Yahweh's
peculiar home. Ezekiel solved it by painting this
unrelieved picture of Israel's sordid career of vice,
which at last provoked Yahweh to the decisive act,
that, for His own sake rather than for hers, He had

so long deferred. There is thus no dark mystery in Israel's suffering, her sin has merited it long ago. The only cause for wonder is that Yahweh has spared her so often. It has not been through any compassion for Israel, but lest His reputation among the heathen should be lowered by His apparent inability to protect the people whom He had chosen for His own. This motive had now ceased to operate as a restraint, for not only had Israel's sin at length become intolerable, but it was injuring His fame among the heathen. Whether He punished or whether He forbore, His reputation must suffer. Accordingly He must first punish Israel for profaning His holy Name before the nations; then He must restore Israel to prove that the exile was not due to His weakness, but was a penalty decreed by His anger. Since the exultation of the heathen over Israel's woes wounded the honour of Israel's God, punishment must be inflicted on them. So determined, in fact, is Yahweh to leave nothing undone, which would enhance His glory, that when Israel is in its own land, He fulfils the old prophecies on the Scythians by dangling the defencelessness of His people as a bait to lure Gog from the land of Magog to attack Israel, to his own ruin. For Yahweh works to magnify His own great Name by a complete destruction of Gog's innumerable hordes, while Israel lifts no finger save to bury the slain and burn their armour and weapons. Thus Yahweh magnifies Himself and sanctifies Himself, and makes Himself known in the eyes of many nations. But while the nations are exterminated that Yahweh may be glorified, Israel's sufferings have become a thing of

the past. Not that this nation has deserved better
treatment than the others. But neither was it restored
mainly because it was Yahweh's favourite. ' Not
for your sake do I this, saith the Lord Yahweh,
be it known unto you : be ashamed and confounded
for your ways, O house of Israel ' (Ezekiel 36[32]).
Here, as everywhere, the all-sufficient motive for
His action is a jealous regard for His own holy Name,
and a desire to get Himself honour in the sight of
the nations.

To our Christian sentiment, Ezekiel seems in many
ways so alien, that it is with difficulty that we can
bring ourselves to do him justice. Awed by the
majesty of Yahweh, crushed by the consciousness
of human frailty, he knows nothing of the glad
freedom of the children of God, of rapturous communion or unspeakable peace. He seems to set
on the throne of the universe a self-centred egoist,
who bends the whole course of history to magnify
His own holy Name. We also think that God has
made us for Himself, yet not for His own sake,
since there is no self-seeking in Him, but because
He knows that He is Himself our highest good.
While the very loftiness of our conception of God's
love makes all the darker the mystery of the world's
pain, it is clear that from Ezekiel's standpoint this
problem could hardly arise.   Man has no case to
plead against God. Yet it is well to be cautious in
judging the prophet. To say that his teaching
must be pronounced very inadequate from a
Christian standpoint is a mere truism.   How could
it be anything else ? Even the sharp exaggeration
and one-sidedness in his doctrine of God and of
individual responsibility do not warrant us in

passing a censure. For revelation is often not so much the expression of absolute truth, as of the truth specially adapted to the needs of those who received it. A one-sided emphasis may have been needed to correct exaggeration in the opposite direction. Whatever defect we may recognize from the Christian point of view, it must be admitted that what saved the religion of Israel from dissolution by the subtle penetrating atmosphere of Greek thought and life, was the hard legalistic rind that protected it, which it owed to Ezekiel more than to any other man.

CHAPTER THREE

The Servant of Yahweh

AN interval of about a quarter of a century
elapsed between the time when we lose sight
of Ezekiel, and the time when the Second Isaiah
began his work. Although the exiles seem to have
been granted considerable freedom, yet it is clear from
the passionate hate of Babylon, which animates the
prophecies of her downfall, even more than from the
specific allusions to oppression, that they suffered no
little from their heathen masters. They had sunk
into a dull acquiescence, dismayed by the might of
Babylon, overwhelmed by the magnificence of her
gods. Yahweh had forgotten His city and His
people, and left them naked to the scorn of their
enemies. Prophets had foretold the rise of their
avenger, and the speedy downfall of their oppressor.
Yet they had not lifted them from their listlessness,
or succeeded in quickening the hope that had died
in their breast. But now their words seemed to find
a justification in the march of events. Cyrus had
begun his career of conquest, and though as yet the
exiles could not believe that the great empire
which held them as its thralls was destined to its
swift destruction, a few prescient souls divined that
in Cyrus the word, which cannot return to Yahweh
void, was effecting its own fulfilment.

Among these was the author, to whom we owe

Isaiah 40-55, one of Israel's greatest prophets, one of the world's chief masters in literature. The Second Isaiah, for so he is usually called, since his name is unknown, bids his people rouse themselves from their despondency. He strikes the keynote of his prophecy in its lovely opening, the music of which still echoes in the English translation : ' Comfort ye, comfort ye my people, saith your God. Speak ye to the heart of Jerusalem, and cry unto her that her warfare is accomplished, that her iniquity is pardoned : that she hath received at Yahweh's hand double for all her sins ' (Isaiah 40$^{1-2}$). It is not necessary for me to linger over some of his great doctrines : his magnificent vindication of Yahweh as the only God, proved by His power to predict, and therefore to control the future, the lofty descriptions of His government in Nature and History, His graciousness in pardon, His tenderness to the weak. All these thoughts are set forth with a wonderful combination of sweetness and force. But these are not the deepest, as they are not the original element in his prophecy. That is to be found in his treatment of the hard problem of Israel's suffering, and his great conception of the Servant of Yahweh. The keenest controversy of recent times in the interpretation of the Old Testament has raged now for several years about the figure of the Servant. The view here adopted is that the Servant of Yahweh is not an individual but the Israelitish nation. It is desirable to reserve the discussion of the views, which have been recently put forward, and the defence of the view here adopted for the Appendix, and to assume here the results, which I shall there seek to make good. I assume, further, as probable, though not demon-

strated, that the four so-called ' Servant of Yahweh
poems' (42^{1-4}, 49^{1-6}, 50^{4-9}, $52^{13}-53^{12}$) were inserted
in their present position by the Second Isaiah him-
self, and were his own composition, though written
perhaps somewhat earlier.

The prophet accepts the sin of Israel as a partial
explanation of its suffering (40^2, 42^{24-5}, 43^{22-8}, 50^1)
and attributes its punishment to Yahweh's wrath
(42^{25}, 47^6, 51^{17-23}, 54^{6-9}). He even reminds us of
Ezekiel in the assertion that it is for the sake of His
Name that Yahweh does not execute the extreme
penalty upon His people (48^{9-11}). Yet his thought
dwells far more on Yahweh's love and His pardoning
grace, displayed in the redemption of Israel from
Babylon. In language of great beauty he again
and again thrills his readers with the outpourings of
Yahweh's affection for Zion and for Israel. Zion
may say ' Yahweh has forgotten me ', and Israel
may utter the hopeless lament : 'My way is hid from
the Lord and my judgement is passed away from my
God.' But though a mother may forget her child,
He cannot forget Zion. She is graven on the palms
of His hands and her walls are ever before Him.
Tempest-tossed and disconsolate, Jerusalem shall
yet arise from the dust, and put on her beautiful
array, shall be established in righteousness, and her
walls shall flash with the fire of precious stones. Other
nations shall be the ransom price for Israel, the
divorced wife shall return to her husband, the
bereaved mother see with glad amazement a multi-
tude of children. The old transgressions shall be
cancelled, and Israel shall be saved with an everlasting salvation. Far from all oppression and terror,
upheld and comforted by Yahweh, she is to be

gathered with great mercies, and with everlasting kindness He will have compassion on her.

Along with all the splendid assertions of monotheism, which have given such lustre to the prophecy, the reader finds other elements logically incompatible with monotheism, but characteristic of a religion which sank from its loftiest flights of universalism into a narrow nationalism. Paul's deduction of universalism from the unity of God, that if God is one, He must be the God of Gentile as well as Jew (Romans 3²⁹⁻³⁰), was not indeed foreign to this prophet's thought. But he had not grasped all that was involved in it, that there is no respect of nations with God, that He can have no favourite people. Hence his doctrine that Egypt, Ethiopia, and Seba, were to be given as a ransom for Israel, that their labours and merchandise should become its possession, that the nations should bring back the exiles, that kings should be their nursing fathers and queens their nursing mothers, that they should bow down to Israel with their faces to the earth, and lick the dust of its feet. Yet when we remember how deeply ingrained in the Jewish people was the misinterpretation of its election, as an end in itself rather than as a means to the world's highest good, we shall wonder less at his assertion of Yahweh's favouritism to His chosen Servant, than at the large-hearted conception of Israel's mission to the Gentiles.

While it is in the Servant passages already mentioned, that this thought of Israel's relation to the heathen is most prominent, at once the explanation of its undeserved suffering, and the motive for its restoration yet in the rest of Isaiah 40–55, whether the author be the author of the Servant passages or not,

Israel's mission to the heathen is a leading idea.
Yahweh bids all the ends of the earth look unto Him
and be saved, and declares that to Him every knee
shall bow, every tongue shall swear. This is to be
accomplished through the glorious restoration of
Israel, at which kings and princes shall arise and
worship. Thus Israel becomes a light to the Gentiles,
Yahweh's witness to the peoples. 'Behold thou
shalt call a nation that thou knowest not, and a
nation that knew not thee shall run unto thee,
because of Yahweh thy God, and for the Holy One
of Israel; for He hath glorified thee' (55[5]). 'Lo,
these shall come from far: and lo, these from the
North and from the West; and these from the land
of Sinim' (49[12]). In Wellhausen's words: 'There
is no God but Yahweh, and Israel is His prophet.'

It is in the light of this mission to the heathen that
Israel's election to be Yahweh's Servant must be
interpreted. Ten or twelve times, apart from the
four Servant passages, Israel is described as Yahweh's
Servant,[a] and often we have some such phrase as
'Thou, Israel, my servant, Jacob, whom I have
chosen'. In the far-off past, Yahweh had laid hold
of the nation and called it from the ends of the earth.
The nation has not always been faithful to its vocation, it has been as unobservant of Yahweh's doing
as if it had been blind, as inattentive to His voice as
if it had been deaf. But now Yahweh has pardoned
the sin of His people, and for its redemption has
raised up Cyrus, through whom its glorious restoration
is to be accomplished.

[a] 41[8-9], 42[19], 43[10], 44[1-2, 21], 45[4], 48[20], 50[10]. The last of these is
doubtful, as there are strong reasons for regarding 50[10-11] as a later
appendix to the third Servant passage. The Servant in 50[10] seems,
in fact, to be an individual prophet.

Our special problem, however, emerges only very slightly in the main portion of Isaiah 40–55, whereas the four Servant passages contain some of the weightiest contributions in the Old Testament toward its solution. It is very unfortunate that the latter part of chapter 53 is so deeply corrupt, that we cannot feel at all sure what the original text was. At the same time the leading ideas are still sufficiently clear.

In the first of these passages (42^{1-4}) Yahweh is the speaker. He introduces the Servant as one whom He holds firmly in His hand, as His chosen in whom He takes delight. Then we learn how he has been prepared for his work—Yahweh has put His Spirit upon him, and what the mission entrusted to him is—to bring to the heathen a knowledge of the true religion. Yahweh next describes the quiet methods he adopts in his teaching ; unlike the older prophets, he will not loudly proclaim his message in the public ways. And he will be gentle in his treatment of the faintest spark of good or truth in the heathen. He will go steadfastly forward with his mission, until he has established the true religion among the heathen, who are already waiting for his instruction

In the second passage (49^{1-6}) the Servant is himself the speaker. He bids the distant heathen nations hearken, and tells them how Yahweh has chosen him from his birth, prepared him for his prophetic work, kept him in His protection, till the time was ripe, and announced to him his call to be His servant, through whom He would win Himself glory. Looking back over his career, the Servant confesses his failure, nevertheless expresses his confidence in God. Now Yahweh, who called him from his birth to be

His servant, has told him, that to bring back Israel from exile is too slight a work for Him to accomplish, so He will make the Servant a light of the nations, that His salvation may be to the ends of the earth.

In the third passage (50^{4-9}) the Servant is again the speaker. It is true that the Servant is not named, but the poem must belong to the cycle of Servant passages, on account of its close affinities with the other members of the group. It is needed, in fact, to form the transition from the two earlier poems, in which the servant is simply the teacher of the nations, to the last passage 52^{13}–53^{12}, in which the martyrdom and exaltation of the Servant are the main theme. The Servant begins his soliloquy with a description of his close relation to Yahweh, who has given him ' the tongue of disciples ', that is the faculty of trained speech, by which he can utter the needful word. Yahweh Himself is his instructor, and every morning reveals His message to him, not in night visions, but in his waking hours. This message he has loyally accepted, though it has brought him cruel indignity and punishment, which he has patiently endured ; not flinching from the task appointed to him. For Yahweh is his helper, therefore he felt no shame, and set his face resolutely like a flint, to accomplish his work. Strong in the assurance that God is his vindicator, he boldly challenges any adversary to contend with him. Since Yahweh has become his helper, he confidently anticipates the destruction of his foes.

The fourth passage (52^{13}–53^{12}) is by far the most important, but also the most difficult. The text is in places very corrupt, so much so in the latter part of chapter 53, that it is impossible to restore it with any confidence. It is also unfortunate that the division of chapters, perhaps never so disastrous as here, has been so effected as to conceal from the ordinary reader that the poem begins with 52^{13} not with 53^{1}. The unique place that the passage holds in the affections of Christendom has tended to emphasize the view that chapter 53 is complete in itself. It should also be added that the current Christian interpretation, however just may be the application of the chapter to Christ, has disguised the fact from the vast majority of readers, that this was not the application in the mind of the writer, who meant Israel by the Servant.

The passage opens with Yahweh's prediction of His Servant's approaching exaltation. Just as many had turned with abhorrence from his countenance, disfigured so as to seem no longer human, so many nations will be startled and kings dumb with amazement at this unexpected elevation. By a fine transition the prophet introduces a confession by the nations, heightening the effect by leaving the identity of the speakers to be inferred. Amazed at the wondrous tidings of the Servant's exaltation they burst into speech with the question : ' Who could have believed that which we have heard ? ' But how were they to know that this glorious destiny was reserved for Israel, since Yahweh's wonder-working power had not before been revealed to them? And while they had received no intimation of this splendid reverse of fortune that awaited him, the previous career of the Servant amply excused their failure to forecast his future. His origin was poor and contemptible, he grew up before his fellow nations like a dwarfed plant in a barren soil. Men found nothing attractive in him, but rather despised and forsook him, for he was smitten with a disease, whose ravages made his appearance so repulsive that men turned in loathing from him. Now the nations confess how utterly they had misconceived the truth. While they looked on the Servant as proved by his sufferings to be an exceptional victim of Divine wrath, it was their own pain and sickness that he was enduring. Their rebellion caused his suffering, his chastisement procured their peace and wrought out their healing. They had gone astray in self-will, and Yahweh had inflicted on him the penalty of their sin. With lamb-like meekness he endured oppression, and was taken away without justice, while none pondered on his fate, that he was smitten to death for the sin of the nations. After his death he was buried in a dishonoured grave, though he was innocent of violence or deceit. So men had judged, but Yahweh judged otherwise. He justified His Servant and delivered him from trouble, satisfied him with a long-lived posterity. In the eyes of the nations the Servant shall be justified, since he has borne their sins. Thus springing out of his career of sacrifice and vicarious atonement, though that career seemed to close in ignominy and death, will come the Servant's exaltation, when restored to life he becomes the equal of the great rulers of the world.

The following translation is offered as representing something like the original Hebrew text of the four passages, though in some cases we are reduced to quite uncertain restoration.

I. ISAIAH 42[1-4]

Lo! my Servant,[b] whom I hold fast,[c]

My chosen, in whom my soul hath pleasure ;

I have put my spirit upon him,

Judgement[d] will he bring forth to the nations.

He will not cry nor lift up,[e]

And he will not make his voice heard in the street.

A bruised reed he will not break,

And a glimmering wick he will not quench.[f]

To the peoples[g] he will bring forth judgement,

---

[b] The LXX reads here, ' Jacob, my Servant,' and in the next line ' Israel, my chosen '. This is correct as an interpretation, but is probably an insertion under the influence of 44[1], 45[4], cf. 41[8], where the names occur in an inverse order. The insertion here disturbs the rhythm.

[c] cf. 41[10], where Israel is similarly described.

[d] Judgement means here the whole complex of religious ordinances, hence like the similar use of the Arabic *din*, as the commentators remind us, is equivalent to the true religion.

[e] ' Lift up,' i.e. lift up his voice. Some read *yish'ag* ' will roar ' instead of *yissa'*, but, as Giesebrecht objects, the word seems too strong. The contrast is often supposed to be with the more demonstrative character of earlier prophecy. This suits an individual better than a national interpretation, and we should probably think of Israel as fulfilling its vocation for the world by quiet missionary activity, not by participation in the politics of great empires. The Servant, as Marti says, follows the method of his Lord, whose working is beautifully compared by Isaiah to ' the waters of Shiloah that go softly (7[6]). Nevertheless, since the author conceived of Israel as Yahweh's prophet to the world, there seems to be no reason why the form of his description may not have been determined by a tacit contrast to the shrill utterances of the prophets in the crowded streets.

[f] Since the Servant has no function to fulfil except for the heathen, the meaning is that he will cherish and strengthen the faint sparks of truth which are to be found among them ; there is no reference to any efforts to rekindle the smouldering flame of truth or goodness in Israel.

[g] The pointed text reads *le'ĕmeth*, which should probably be translated ' in accordance with truth '. But it is better to alter the pointing with Giesebrecht, and read *le'ummōth* ' to the peoples '. We thus get a correspondence with verse 1, ' Judgement will he bring forth to the nations.'

He will not glimmer nor be crushed,[h]
Till he set judgement in the earth,
And for his teaching the far lands wait [i]

II.   ISAIAH 49[1-6]

Hearken ye far lands to me,
And listen ye distant peoples :
Yahweh hath called me from my birth,
From my mother's womb hath He made mention
    of my name.

And He made my mouth like a keen blade,
In the shadow of His hand He hid me,
And He made me a polished arrow,[j]
In His quiver He concealed me.

And He said to me ' Thou art my servant,
Israel,[k] in whom I will get myself glory '
But I said ' In vain have I toiled,

[h] For *yāruts* we should with Ewald and many others, following
the Codex Babylonicus, read *yerōts* (Imperfect niphal of *ratsats*).

[i] The last line is not a continuation of the preceding, dependent on
' till '. It is an independent sentence asserting that the heathen are
already eagerly desiring the truth, which the Servant is to bring them,
a thought for which the preceding verse prepares us.   For this
wonderfully liberal estimate of the heathen we may compare
Malachi 1[11], and the beautiful description of their willingness to
receive the truth, given in the Book of Jonah.

[j] This is the usual translation, but Buhl (Gesenius-Buhl *sub voce*)
thinks it means ' sharpened arrow '.

[k] Duhm, of course, strikes out ' Israel ' as an incorrect gloss.
Even some of those who accept the identification of the Servant with
Israel admit that this is possible even if not probale (so Skinner,
Marti, and Giesebrecht, the last of these thinking that there may be
an intentional mystery hanging over the identification of the Servant).
There is no solid reason whatever for assuming it to be a gloss, unless
we adopt the view that the Servant is an individual.   The balance of
clauses is disturbed by its removal.   All the versions read it, and it is
omitted only in one Hebrew MS. (Kennicott 96). Giesebrecht thinks
the whole of verse 3 may be an insertion.   His reasons are not conclusive, they are stated in a footnote on page 49 of his *Der Knecht
Jahves.*

Idly and to no purpose have I exhausted my strength :
Nevertheless my right is with Yahweh,
And my reward with my God '
And now saith Yahweh—
Who formed me from the womb to be His Servant,
To bring back Jacob to Himself,
And that Israel might be gathered to Him,[1]
And I was honoured in the eyes of Yahweh,

[1] 49[5-6] has been a stronghold of those who hold that the Servant
cannot be identified with the empirical Israel, since in these verses
they seem to be expressly distinguished, and it seems to be affirmed
that part of the Servant's mission is to restore Israel from exile.
There are weighty antecedent objections to this, which are stated in
the Appendix (pp. 172–3). Yet the passage does not demand this
interpretation, though the immediate impression it makes perhaps
favours it. Yet Duhm, in spite of his vigorous rejection of the national
theory, thinks that there is no reference here to a restoration of Israel
by the Servant. Unfortunately the text of 49[5] is uncertain. It is not
necessary to discuss the text here, since the general sense is plain
that the passage speaks of a bringing back of Israel to Yahweh. The
crucial question is ' Who brings Israel back ? ' Usually it is said that
it is the Servant, in which case a distinction between Israel and the
Servant would seem to be made out. Some scholars, however,
including Duhm, insist that it is Yahweh. This harmonizes much
better with the general language of the prophet, since nowhere else
have we the faintest hint that this function is entrusted to the
Servant. We could accordingly freely translate : ' That he might
bring back Jacob to Himself.' The reference is apparently to the
return from Babylon to Yahweh's land, though Budde ingeniously
refers it to the Exodus, translating : ' In that he brought Jacob again
(out of Egypt) to him, and drew Israel to him (into the desert)'
(American Journal of Theology, iii, 520 = Ebed-Jahwe Lieder, pp. 22–3).
This connects very well with the mention of Israel's call in the
preceding verse, but it is improbable since the reference is surely to
the same event as in verse 6, i.e. the restoration from exile. In any
case there is no need to think of the Servant as restoring Israel, the
contradiction and other difficulties thus created outweighing the
impression which the words themselves most naturally give.
Giesebrecht, however, argues at length and very forcibly that
the two lines translated above, ' To bring back Jacob to Himself and
that Israel might be gathered,' should be struck out as a gloss,
occasioned by the gloss in verse 6 (Der Knecht Jahves, pp. 40–6).
I think that he may quite probably be right, and certainly the present
text is very awkward ; but it is rather drastic treatment, and for our
purpose we may well be content with the result that Yahweh and not
the Servant is represented as restoring Israel.

And my God was my strength—
' Too slight a thing is it to raise up the tribes of
    Jacob,[m]
And to bring back the preserved of Israel,
So I make thee a light of the nations,
That My salvation may be to the ends of the earth.'

III.   ISAIAH 50[4—9]

The Lord Yahweh hath given me
    A disciple's tongue,

[m] The present Hebrew text was, before Dillmann, explained a sin
the translation of the Revised Version : ' It is too light a thing that
thou shouldest be my Servant to raise up the tribes of Jacob, and to
restore the preserved of Israel.'   This clearly means that part of the
Servant's function is to restore Israel from exile. But Dillmann
pointed out in his note on the passage that if the prophet had meant
what earlier commentators had supposed him to mean, the Hebrew
would have been different. We must accordingly translate the present
text with Dillmann : ' Too light a thing for thy being my Servant is it
to raise up the tribes of Jacob and to restore the preserved of Israel.'
This may be explained in two ways : (a) It is not worthy of the Servant's position that he should simply restore Israel from exile ; (b) It
is not worthy of the Servant's position that Yahweh should restore
Israel from exile. But the Hebrew, as thus correctly interpreted, is
very clumsy. Duhm drew what seems to be the necessary inference
that the words ' for thy being my Servant ' are a gloss. In this he has
been followed by Cheyne, Marti, and Giesebrecht. When these words
are struck out, and we translate as above, the passage most naturally
means that Yahweh considers the restoration of Israel from exile too
light a thing for Him to accomplish, so He will make Israel a light to
the nations. The line is virtually equivalent to ' Too slight a thing is it
for Me to raise up the tribes of Jacob'. The gloss probably originated
through a marginal note, intended to explain in what respect the
restoration of Israel was ' too slight a thing'. It was too slight for
the Servant's position as Servant of Yahweh.   When the gloss is
omitted there remains no reason for distinguishing between the
Servant and Israel and supposing that the former has a task to
accomplish for the latter.

That I might know to answer the godless
  With upright words."
In the morning He awakeneth mine ear
  To hear like disciples.
The Lord Yahweh hath opened
  For me the ear.°
And I was not rebellious,
  I turned not backward.ᵖ

---

n The present text is translated in the R.V., ' That I should know how to sustain with words him that is weary'. This is open to serious objections. We have no other occurrence of a verb '*ūth* in Hebrew. If it is correctly read here its meaning can only be conjectured, ' sustain ' or ' refresh ' suits the mention of ' the weary '. The general drift of the passage, however, suggests rather that a mention of the Servant's adversaries should come here instead of the weary. Further, *dābār* should hardly mean ' with words', for this we expect a preposition to be prefixed. The following words are also suspicious (as the insertion of Paseq suggests). They are *yā'īr babbōqer babbōqer yā'īr*, ' he wakeneth in the morning in the morning he wakeneth'. At first sight Duhm's suggestion, accepted by Marti and Cheyne (*Sacred Books of the Old Testament*), that ' he wakeneth in the morning ' should be struck out as incorrect dittography of the following words, seems the best solution. We should, on the whole, however, have expected the words in that case to have been repeated in the same order. It seems plain that the repetition of *babbōqer* ' in the morning' has arisen through dittography, so it may be struck out. We have then to emend the preceding words. For *la'ūth* it is simplest to read with Graetz, followed by Duhm and Giesebrecht (*Der Knecht Jahves*, p. 54), *la'ănōth* ' to answer ' which involves an extremely slight alteration of the Hebrew. For *yā'ēph*, ' the weary ', I have adopted Duhm's suggestion *chānēph*, ' the godless'. There remains *dābār yā'īr*. We can change *yā'īr* into *yāshār*, ' an upright word', or we can read *dibrē yōsher*, ' words of uprightness', assuming that the *yod* at the end of the first word has fallen out because the next word began with it. This is the emendation adopted above.

o Duhm, followed by Cheyne and Marti, omits this couplet as a variant of the clause ' in the morning he wakeneth mine ear ' in the preceding verse. Perhaps the connexion is improved by the omission, but there is no decisive reason for it.

p The Servant asserts his loyal acceptance of Yahweh's message. It is quite possible that the author of the Book of Jonah had this passage in his mind when he represented Israel as refusing the mission to which God had called her through the Second Isaiah, to proclaim to the heathen the knowledge of the true God.

[And princes shuddered at him],
(For marred so as not to be human was his visage,
And his form so as not to be that of the sons of men),
So shall he startle*w* many nations,
At him kings shall shut their mouths,
For what was not told them they see,
And what they did not hear they consider.

w This is a famous *crux*. The word *yazzeh* is Hiphil of *nāzāh*. It
is used elsewhere only in the sense of sprinkling a liquid in ceremonial
acts. It is not used like the English ' sprinkle ', with an accusative
of the person on whom the liquid is sprinkled. We cannot, therefore,
translate ' so shall he sprinkle many nations '. The only sense we
could impose on the word, if the meaning ' sprinkle ' is retained,
would be that the Servant should scatter nations, as water is scattered
when it is sprinkled. It is generally agreed that this sense is impossible here, straining the language, and out of harmony with the
relations between the Servant and the nations as elsewhere described,
The view now usually taken is that it means ' to cause to spring up'.
' to startle', this sense being derived from the Arabic word *nazâ*, 'to
leap '. I have adopted this in the translation, though with some
misgivings. Cheyne objects that the word is rare in Arabic classical
literature, and that Hebrew has so many words for ' leap ' that it is
unnecessary to have recourse to Arabic. Followed by Marti, he has
suggested *yishtachăwū*, which occurs in the parallel 49[7] : ' So shall
many nations bow down before him.' Moore, followed by Duhm,
reads *yirgezū*, ' shall be moved '.

Giesebrecht is convinced that a line has been lost, but does not
attempt to restore it. I have not followed Marti, however, in
removing the parenthesis. Giesebrecht's objection that it is much
too strong to be appropriate after 53[2] seems to me to be sound. The
real objection to it is not that it is a parenthesis, but that it is introduced by ' so '. Giesebrecht removes this by the very simple remedy
of changing *kēn*, ' so,' into *kî*, ' for ', and I have followed him in my
translation.

'Who could have believed that which we have
    heard ?[x]
But to whom was the arm of Yahweh revealed ?
For he grew up as a sapling before us,[y]
And as a root out of a dry ground,
He had no form that we should look upon him,

[x] At this point the prophet introduces a confession by speakers, who
are left unnamed. This is in accordance with his custom elsewhere,
each of the Servant passages opens without any mention of the speaker.
It is here assumed that the heathen are the speakers ; the reasons for
this conclusion are given in the Appendix (pp. 168–70). For the translation ' Who could have believed ? ' see Giesebrecht, *Beiträge*, p. 159.
Budde, *Ebed Jahwe-Lieder*, p. 14, n. 2, aptly compares *mi millēl*, ' who
would have said ? ' Genesis 21[7]. The expression is probably borrowed from colloquial speech, and is like our phrase ' Who would
have thought it ? ' The translation ' our report ' is very unfortunate.
The nations ask : ' Who could have believed the tidings we have now
heard ? ' In the shock of surprise caused by the Servant's exaltation,
to which reference has just been made, the ' many nations ' break
forth into this expression of their astonishment. There is no real
contradiction between this and the statement that ' kings shall shut
their mouths '. Both convey the same thought, the extreme amazement of the heathen. A poet may in one sentence represent them as
dumb with astonishment, and in the next as uttering that astonishment in speech, without exposing himself to any charge of incon-
sistency, except from very prosaic readers. Nor is the objection,
urged by Professor Skinner, conclusive, that the nations ' are
surprised by the Servant's exaltation because they had not previously
heard of it ; those who now speak confess a deeper fault, they have
heard but did not believe '. The whole tone of what follows appears
to show that the speakers, while confessing their misconception, urge
that there was abundant excuse for it. The second line of 53[1]
accordingly seems to mean that their former attitude to the Servant
was not to be wondered at, since none of them had received any
revelation of the great act Yahweh was about to accomplish.

[y] With Ewald and several others, it is better to read *lephānēynū*,
' before us ', than *lephānāyw*, ' before him ', though Duhm, Skinner,
and Budde still retain the latter. Marti suggests *lephānim*, 'afore-
time '.

Therefore shall he inherit[1] amongst the many,
And with the strong he shall divide the spoil.
Inasmuch as he poured out his soul unto death,
And was numbered with the rebellious,
Though he bore the sin of many,
And interceded for the rebellious.

It is out of the nation's exile that this wonderful
series of poems springs. The prophet ponders deeply
the significance of this dark experience for the nation's
task. What place is he to give it in his theory
of Israel's mission ? He sets out from the conviction
that such a mission has been assigned by Yahweh to
His Servant. What else could be the purpose of
its choice before it had even begun to be ? If it was
Israel that was thus called to be Yahweh's Servant
the mission committed to it could be only a mission
to the world. And we can see how the writer rose
to the great thought that Israel was destined to be
Yahweh's prophet to the Gentiles. In Babylon he
confronted a splendid idolatry, and as he saw the

[1] The LXX reads ' he shall inherit ' instead of ' I will divide '.
With Duhm, Cheyne, and Marti I have adopted this, since the change
from the third person is unlikely, as is also the repetition of the same
verb in the first and second lines.

---

him ', *chāphēts hatsdīqō* for *chāpēts dakke'ō* (the scribe wrote to the
first *ts* and in returning to the text before him started again from the
second).   This is supported by 50[8].   ' Yahweh was pleased to crush
him ' gives a sense quite alien to the passage, and in itself very
unlikely.   Duhm rightly says that the general sense required is,
' While men judged the Servant in the way described, Yahweh
judged otherwise '.   He translates, with the LXX, 'Yahweh was
pleased to purify him ', which can be got out of the present text.
It is perhaps not worth while going through the passage in detail
with a view to emending it.   The reconstructions by Duhm, Cheyne,
and Giesebrecht differ much from that here given and from each other,

people of Yahweh crushed by the heel of the heathen, the iron entered into his soul. Hence the contest between Yahweh and the false gods derived much of its interest for him. He knows that Yahweh is the true God, since He alone predicts, and therefore alone shapes the future. To Him the nations must look, forsaking their senseless idolatry. Since Israel, and no other people, possesses the knowledge of Yahweh, what can its mission be but to make Him known to the world ? Nor are the heathen wholly unprepared. Beneath the loud devotion to their own deities, the prophet's ear has caught the low undertone of a worthier aspiration. Their souls are stirred with a vague disquiet, a dim sense of higher truth, a longing for the ' authentic voice ' to change the soaring wish to a luminous certainty. ' For his teaching the far lands do wait.' Not only, however, has Israel been selected for this vocation, but Yahweh is training His Servant to fulfil it. Equipped with His Spirit, and taught by His own intimate revelations, he knows how to give the right answer, and has learnt a tender respect for the faintest gleams of light that struggle to exist in heathenism. But all this preparation, which has made Israel as fit for its work as a keen blade for battle, seemed now to have been stultified. The nation had been bitterly persecuted, and had lost its life. Ezekiel had already depicted the destruction of Israel's national existence by the exile as a death, and had prophesied that it would be undone in the restoration. The same metaphor is used here to express the same idea. Why then should this strange fate have befallen the Servant ? A partial answer lay ready to hand. The suffering of the Servant was a martyrdom, exclusive, must not lead us too hastily to condemn them. Probably it was inevitable that the ideals of the Second Isaiah, like those of Jeremiah, should wait till their time was ripe. Spiritual religion was as yet too weak for Judaism to take such soaring flights. First of all, it must make its own position secure, then attempt the conquest of the world. The truths, which Jeremiah and the Second Isaiah had taught, lay hidden within that hard shell, and had they not been so protected might have been lost to the world. Yet it can only be with pain that we think how long-continued the exclusiveness of Judaism has been. The author of the Book of Jonah perhaps next to Jeremiah the greatest of the Hebrew Prophets, urged his countrymen to accept the mission to the heathen, and sought to convince them how ready they were for the truth. But his noble protest fell on deaf ears ; his generous estimate of the Gentiles found no echo in the Jewish heart. So when the time came for Judaism frankly to throw off its racial limitations and become a universal religion, it made the great refusal, and Christianity had to develop in almost entire independence of it. Yet it would be unworthy to forget how vast is the debt we owe to Jewish teachers, and how amply the promise that Israel should be a light of the Gentiles has been redeemed.

It is less easy for us to sympathize with the prophet's doctrine that Israel had been the vicarious sufferer for the world's sin. It seems at first sight so out of touch with reality, so calm in its defiance of patent facts. The objection can, indeed, be dealt with only in the light of wider applications of the principle involved in it. It is, however, plain that here the prophet assigned a function to Israel, to which, in the nature of things, a nation is inadequate. It would, I believe, be mistaken to infer from this that he had in mind simply the pious kernal of the nation or the ideal Israel. Each of these is exposed to grave difficulties of an exegetical kind, while they cut the prophecy away from its historical root. Nevertheless, while the Servant is the actual nation, and the exile is the death in which its afflictions have culminated, it is that nation looked at from the point of view of function. Israel is in a measure idealized, since in his absolute way of stating his doctrine, the prophet looks away from the imperfect realization of the function assigned to it, and speaks as if it had completely achieved the ideal which God had set before it.

From the first, Christianity has seen in the description of the Suffering Servant a prediction of Jesus of Nazareth. It is, however, a firmly established result of exegesis that this was not at all in the prophet's mind. He does not intend by the Servant of Yahweh a figure that is to come centuries later than his own time. This Servant has already lived and died, and the prophet utters his oracle after the death, but before the resurrection of the Servant. Moreover, in common with many interpreters, I am convinced that he intends by the Servant, not an individual at all but the Israelitish nation, though several scholars do not accept this view. Are we, then, to say that the Church has been wrong in its interpretation ? I have already said that a nation could not be adequate to the functions here assigned to the Servant. We may solve the difficulty if we can identify Jesus with Israel.

Israel is now treading that ninth circle of the Saint's Inferno. Yahweh has abandoned him, He is far from his cry[m] and the words of his roaring. Yet Israel still cleaves fast to Him, and begins the invocation with the pathetic repetition, 'My God, my God.' He cries by day and receives no answer, by night and obtains no relief. How strange that he should need to cry 'Why hast Thou forsaken me?' that he should appeal for help in his extremity in vain! For Yahweh is the Holy One, pledged by His holiness to save His people. Nay, more, He is enthroned on the praises of Israel,[n] so that if these are silenced through Israel's destruction, Yahweh's exaltation by men comes to an end. Individuals may perish, and Yahweh's praise still go on as before, but if the nation dies, His service can no longer be maintained. The fathers trusted in Him, and He did not disappoint their trust, but when they cried to Him they were delivered. But now how different is the lot of their descendants. Israel is

[m] The text reads, 'from my salvation', *mishu'āthi*. The versions translated the line ' far from my salvation are the words of my roaring', and among modern scholars this is adopted by Baethgen. The meaning would be that the sufferer's cries are far from his Saviour, i.e. Yahweh. The expression is rather unnatural, and the translation, ' Being far from my salvation and the words of my roaring', yields a better sense. The Hebrew, however, is hardly what we should have expected, and it is better with Hitzig and several other scholars to make a very slight change in the text and read *mishshaw'āthi*, ' from my cry'. Bickell, Cheyne, and Duhm emend more radically.

[n] A beautiful transformation of the older thought of God as enthroned on the cherubim. I think the meaning of the passage which springs from its position in the context is that indicated above. But I must give myself the pleasure of quoting Prof. Cheyne's exquisite paraphrase in the Introduction to his *Commentary* : ' These Spirit-taught utterances of the heart can like the " throne-bearing " cherubim at any moment bring him nigh.'

a mere worm,[o] the by-word of the heathen, exposed to their contempt.[p] Jeeringly the heathen say : ' Yahweh is his redeemer,[q] let Him rescue him ; let Him deliver him, for He has pleasure in him.' Yet from his earliest infancy[r] Yahweh had been his confidence and sustainer ; let Him draw near, for he is in peril and their is none to help. The sufferer now describes the attack of the heathen nations. They have hemmed him in like wild beasts, the dogs

[o] The reference is to Isaiah 41[14] : ' Fear not, thou worm Jacob, and ye men of Israel ; I will help thee, saith Yahweh, and thy redeemer is the Holy One of Israel.' There are other echoes of this passage in the Psalm.

[p] cf. Isaiah 53[3], 49[7].

[q] The text reads *gōl'el Yahweh*, ' roll unto Yahweh'. The meaning is thought to be Roll thy care on Yahweh. It is much better to accept Halévy's suggestion, which is adopted by Cheyne, *gō'lăō Yahweh*, ' his redeemer is Yahweh'. The alteration is slight and the sense much improved. The point of the taunt is much sharper if the heathen are quoting Israel's own words, or the words of Yahweh about Israel, and it is common in the Second Isaiah to find Yahweh thus spoken of as Israel's *gō'ēl*. So in 41[14], the passage already mentioned, but also 43[14], 44[6, 24], 47[4], 48[17], 49[7, 26], 54[5, 8]. We should also not forget the famous passage in Job, ' I know that my *gō'ēl* liveth'. The reference to the Servant in Isaiah 40–55 is further emphasized by the closing words of the sentence, ' He has pleasure in Him', which reminds us of Isaiah 42[1], and, if Marti's reading in 53[10] is correct, ' But Yahweh had pleasure in His Servant', of that passage also.

[r] Here again there are references to the Servant in the Second Isaiah, 46[3], 44[2, 24], 49[1, 5]. If, as some think, there is a reference to the custom of laying the new-born child before the father, that he might acknowledge it by taking it on his knees, or disown it by leaving it to lie, Duhm's suggestion that for '*ēlī*, ' my God ', we should read '*ābī*, ' my father', deserves consideration. Israel's sonship and Yahweh's fostering care in the infancy of the nation is a familiar thought in the Old Testament.

tear gaping wounds in his hands and feet.[s]   His
vital powers ebb away, his bones are wrenched out of
joint, his heart fails him, his palate[t] is parched.   He
is drawing near to death, and it is Yahweh who is
bringing him down to the dust of death.   Behind
the instrument He stands as the efficient cause.
The victim is worn to a skeleton, his enemies gaze
with delight on his suffering, and are so sure of his
death that they do not wait for it before they appor-
tion his garments among them.   Once more he urges
Yahweh to come to his help, to deliver his life from
the sword; already he is in the lion's jaws, and prays
to be delivered.   He continues his prayer, ' And
from the horns of the wild oxen ', but just as he is
about to complete it, in a sudden inspiration of faith
he soars into the triumphant assurance that God has

---

[s] Wellhausen's rearrangement, by which verse 16 follows on verse
12, seems a distinct improvement.   The line translated in the E.V.,
' They pierced my hands and my feet', is in the Hebrew, as pointed,
' Like a lion my hands and my feet',   This is unintelligible, and even
if we supply some such words as ' they tore ', it is not clear why hands
and feet should be mentioned, as a lion does not select these for
attack. The LXX, Vulgate, and Syriac, read *ka'ărŭ*, ' they dug',
instead of *ka'ărĭ*, ' like a lion'.   The passage should then be explained as above. The translation ' they pierced ' is unjustifiable.
It is probably a case of fitting Old Testament language to what was
supposed to be New Testament fulfilment.   But the passage is
not quoted in the New Testament, which does not, in fact, speak
of the feet of Jesus as pierced, though such a reference is possible
in Luke 24[39].   The best translation is ' they have dug into my
hands and feet'.   This is not quite natural, and possibly the text
is corrupt.   Wellhausen translates ' my hands and feet like a lion',
and thinks the line has no intelligible meaning here, and has come
in by pure accident. If not original, verse 13 may be partly
responsible for its insertion.

[t] The text reads *kōchĭ*, ' my strength', but we should, with many
scholars, read *chikkĭ*, ' my palate', as much more suitable to the
context.

heard him, and breaks off with the exclamation :
' Thou hast answered me.'[u] It is now fitting that he
should burst into praise for his deliverance, and this
follows in the closing portion of the Psalm. The
text is unfortunately not certain in some places, but
for our purpose it is not necessary to follow the Psalm
further in detail. The most important feature is
that the deliverance of Israel has for its issue the
conversion of the heathen.

The Psalm contributes nothing toward a solution
of the problem. It has no hint to give which would
explain the mystery of Israel's dark experience.
But it has its own value, in that it is a cry out
of the depths, uttered by a people that in the
bitterest trouble holds fast to God, even when the
extreme pain befalls it of the hiding of God's face.
From this deep despondency springs an expression
of thanksgiving for deliverance. It is not that
deliverance has already come, but that faith has
triumphed over the certainties of the world, and the
apparent indifference of God. And in that marvellous assurance the sufferer, still ringed with relentless
foes, with his life-blood ebbing away, and God
seeming deaf to his cry, wins that serene confidence,
which lifts him above his pain, above the certainty

---

[u] We should have expected the couplet to be completed : And
from the horns of the wild oxen do thou deliver me.' The change
from this to the unexpected assertion of deliverance, in our present
text, is very fine and effective. Some, however, are not satisfied
with it. Wellhausen, adopting a suggestion of Thrupp's, corrects
'*ănīthānī*, 'thou hast answered me', into '*ănīyāthī*, which he translates
'my miserable life'. He thus gets as in 25[16] a parallel to 'my only one',
which occurs in the last line of the preceding couplet. Duhm
reads '*ozrēnī*, ' help me'.

of impending death, and fills him with the sublime
conviction that he shall yet live and declare the
wonderful works of God. And with his faith there
is joined a noble charity, too rare in the utterance of
oppressed Psalmists. These heathen nations that
have well-nigh brought Israel to its death stir within
him no unholy passion for revenge. They are, on the
contrary, to receive the lofty privilege of becoming
Yahweh's worshippers. ' All the ends of the earth
shall remember and turn unto Yahweh ; and all the
kindreds of the nations shall worship before Thee.'

CHAPTER FOUR

A Century of Disillusion

THE second Isaiah had painted in glowing colours the release of the Jews from captivity, their happy return to Palestine, with the privations of the march miraculously removed, the splendours of Zion, the brilliant future of the restored community. But the Jews did not respond to the privilege accorded them by Cyrus in 536 B.C., and but few abandoned their homes in the land, where they had so deeply struck their roots, to face the perils of the forgotten and desolate land of their fathers. The return to Palestine was never, indeed, within measurable distance of being accomplished, and prophets long cherished the ideal of a complete gathering to Canaan of all the Jews in the Dispersion. Those who returned soon found that the enchanting prospects which had lured them to Zion, gave place to cruel disillusion. Bad harvests, drought, and the general wretchedness of their conditions quickly chilled their enthusiasm. They had come intending to rebuild the temple. But they delayed, feeling that in their misery the time was not auspicious. The prophets, Haggai and Zechariah, urged them to the work, promising a happy change of fortune if they let Yahweh's house lie waste no longer. They traced their accumulated misfortunes to their neglect of Yahweh and preference of their own interests. When the prophets had secured the obedience of the community, and it was disheartened with the inferiority of the new temple to the old, they took up the promises of the Second Isaiah, and predicted a splendid future. For soon Yahweh will convulse the earth, and in the crash of empires the Messianic age shall dawn, and the desirable things of the nations shall stream into Jerusalem. Thus the glory of the latter house shall be greater than the glory of the former. And for Zerubbabel an illustrious destiny is reserved : ' In that day, saith Yahweh of hosts, will I take thee, O Zerubbabel my servant, the son of Shealtiel, saith Yahweh, and will make thee as a signet : for I have chosen thee saith Yahweh of hosts ' (Haggai 2^{23}). It is probable that in the original text of Zechariah 6$^{9-15}$, the prophet spoke of a command he had received to crown Zerubbabel.)

The crash of the Persian empire was not, however, to come as yet. Its fall seemed not improbable, for in the year before Haggai and Zechariah came forward, almost the whole empire, though not Syria or Asia Minor, was in revolt. The insurrections were suppressed, and the empire lasted for nearly two hundred years longer. It is an interesting question whether Zerubbabel was tempted to participate in a Messianic revolt, and lost his position or even his life in consequence. That his later history is quite unknown to us suggests that he may have fallen into disfavour at the Persian court, though even his deposition and still more his execution, perhaps by crucifixion, remains at best a conjecture. Its interest for us lies partly in the deepening of the gloom in Judah and the reaction from the Messianic hopes which the contemporary prophets had so brightly portrayed, partly in the suggestion that Zerubbabel is the suffering servant of Isaiah 52^{13}–53^{12} which has been recently revived by Sellin and Kittel, though the former of these has still more recently withdrawn his name in favour of Jehoiachin. It is unnecessary for me to discuss it, since the view is excluded if I am right in thinking that the Servant is not an individual but the nation.

Before leaving Zechariah, I must refer to the remarkable passage with which the third chapter of his prophecy opens. Joshua the high priest is standing before Yahweh in filthy garments, and at his right hand stands the Satan to contest his plea. The thought is probably that the high priest's filthy garments symbolize the sin of the community of which he is the representative ; though not sin which still remains to be atoned for, since otherwise Yahweh could hardly have implied by His rebuke to the Satan that the accusation he was urging against Joshua was unjust. In the fact of its misery the Satan, who here expresses the judgement of the traditional theology, sees an evidence of its guilt, and thus disputes the standing of its representative before God. This is a reflection of the view that the people must have taken of their misfortunes. They argued, we are wretched, therefore Yahweh is angry with us for our sin. They doubted whether God would renew His favour, or, as the prophet would say, whether the Satan would establish his case against them before God. The vision corrects this misgiving. Had the Satan won his case, the miseries of Judah would have continued. But Yahweh decides against him and rebukes him, He has plucked Jerusalem as a brand from the

seemed to have returned, and an attitude was
assumed to the problem of suffering similar to what
we find in Job, though, of course, in a much more
superficial form.   There was a deep scepticism as
to Yahweh's moral government.   The prophet
quotes a current saying : ' Every one that doeth evil
is good in the sight of Yahweh, and He delighteth in
them ' (2^{17}).   Even the pious had given way to
despondency : ' It is in vain to serve God, and what
profit is it that we have kept His charge, and that
we have walked mournfully before Yahweh of
Hosts ?   And now we call the proud happy ; yea,
they that work wickedness are built up ; yea, they
tempt God and are delivered.'   There is no solution,
but simply a reproof for wearying God and uttering
stout words against Him, and a prediction that the
day of Yahweh is soon coming, when the wicked will
be punished and the God-fearing will be spared, and
the difference will be clearly seen between the
righteous and the evil-doers.

A few years later, in the time of Ezra and Nehemiah,
we may place the greater part of Isaiah 56–66.   It is
hard to believe that Duhm and Marti are right in
assigning the whole of these eleven chapters to a single
hand.   It is a strain on our natural disinclination to
analysis when we find the levels in its various parts
so different.   Can the author of 60–2 have written
anything else in these chapters ?   Moreover, 63^7–64^{12}
surely cannot in the face of 64^{11} have been written in
the age of Nehemiah, when a temple was actually in
existence ; Duhm's reply, that this temple is passed
over as unworthy of mention in comparison with
Solomon's, being very unsatisfactory.   It would be
simplest to date it during the exile, while the first

temple lay in ashes, and the second had not risen on its site, were it not for the words, 'Thy holy people possessed it but a little while'. If we could confidently accept Robertson Smith's theory that the Elohistic Psalms, usually supposed to spring from the darkest period of the persecution by Antiochus Epiphanes, really belonged to the time of Artaxerxes Ochus, about the middle of the fourth century, it would be natural to follow Cheyne in assigning this section to the same time. If, in the silence of history, this be thought too precarious, we should do better to revert to an exilic date, rather than bring it down to the Maccabean period. With this exception, however, it is probable that the whole of Isaiah 56–66 belongs to the age of Nehemiah. Yet while these chapters cast a welcome light on the material welfare of the people and their religious, moral, and social condition, they say little that is of value for our purpose. But they confirm the impression, already derived from Malachi, of the disillusion that prevailed toward the end of a century, which opened with such dazzling prospects. The community, whose glorious destiny the Second Isaiah had foretold with such rapturous eloquence, was as far from attaining it as could well be imagined. All the evils which the old prophets had denounced seemed to fester in it, and fully explained the misfortunes by which it was overwhelmed. The rulers are greedy and drunken. There is a zealous religionism, which finds expression in fasting, but which is unavailing in God's sight. For while they sit in sackcloth and ashes with bowed heads, they fast for strife and to smite with the fist or wickedness, and oppress their labourers. They wonder that

of heaven, and he himself lives in the consciousness of unbroken communion with God. Now the
Satan, whose function was to detect the evil that
lurked beneath the show of virtue, has in the
zealous discharge of his duty found that apparent
virtue is so often the disguise of vice, that he has
become the victim of a cynicism too hardened to
admit that any man can really be virtuous unless
God makes it worth his while. To turn His zealous
servant from so unjust an estimate. Yahweh
challenges his cynicism with the case of Job. The
Satan is ready with his reply. He had left no stone
unturned to unmask piety so conspicuous, and had
been forced to admit the genuineness of Job's
virtue. But, granted that Job is no hypocrite,
is his virtue worth anything after all ? Who would
not be virtuous, when virtue paid so well ? So the
Satan meets Yahweh's challenge with another
Strip Job of his wealth and bereave him of his
children, and he will fawn on Yahweh no longer,
but curse Him to His face. So, with Yahweh's
permission, Job by a series of appalling catastrophes
is robbed in one day of property and children.
Yet he disappoints his adversary by submitting in
beautiful resignation to the will of heaven, which
as it gives, so also can take away. Foiled in his first
attempt, the Satan is at no loss for a reason. With
the colloquial freedom of an old servant, he tells
Yahweh that a man's own skin is his main concern,
if possessions and family go, he may reckon himself
not so badly off, if he keeps his own skin whole.
Once more with Yahweh's permission, the untiring
sceptic seeks to force curses from Job's lips by rack-
ing him with an intolerable disease. But nobly

patient, the sufferer meets his wife's suggestion of
revolt with one of the classical utterances of resignation : ' Good shall we receive at the hand of God,
and evil shall we not receive ? ' So Job comes
triumphantly out of his trials, and Yahweh's confidence in his Servant's goodness is magnificently
vindicated.

Yet while he holds by his piety and utters from
his heart the language of resignation, the calamity
that crushed him was an inexplicable mystery. The
teaching of his day regarded great misfortune as
a sign of great sin, and an evidence of the anger of
God. Yet he was so conscious of his own uprightness,
so sure moreover of God's favour, that he could not
all at once apply his theology to his own tragic
change of fortune. It is clear that as the logic of
the situation developed, it would be more likely to
shake his faith in God than in his own integrity.
For the latter was certified to him by his own
immediate consciousness, whereas the former was
guaranteed only by the traditional orthodoxy, and
his past experience. And this past experience did
not prove God's goodness, it suggested it, indeed,
but, after all, the happiness he had enjoyed might
only have masked some sinister design. What if
God had planned the catastrophe from the first,
and to make it the more bitter had set him for long
years serenely on the pinnacle of bliss, caressed by
His sunshine and confident in His smile ? As he
brooded, till the weeks stretched into months, on
the strange fate that had surprised him, the doubt
of God's goodness must have stolen into his mind.
Though he would banish it as blasphemy, it must
have forced its way back as often as he repelled it

For, on the facts before him, what other solution
could present itself to one trained to regard great
suffering as branding its victim with the curse of
God ? Sure of his own innocence, what can he say
but this, that the God who smites the innocent with
His curse, must Himself be immoral ? This, then,
is Job's problem, and with its emergence the centre
of interest shifts from the trial to which the Satan
has exposed him, to the conflict within his own soul.
It is just the deep piety of Job that makes the
struggle so intense, nay so terrific. A man, fitted
beyond most to find his happiness in the love of
God, feeling that his confidence in God's righteousness is shattered, we see him driven on till he
defies God because he must be true to himself.
Such is the sublime spectacle the poet has dared to
show us : a weak man, strong in the justice of
his cause, rebuking the Almighty to His face for
His immoral government of the world. It is all the
more sublime that Job is no Stoic. He does not
proudly despise his pain, nor in haughty self-esteem
count himself the equal of the gods. A driven leaf,
a fleeting shadow, quailing before God's majesty,
quivering in agony at the touch of pain, how lofty
the moral courage that impels him to confront God
with nothing but his own rectitude and his burning
hatred of wrong, to dare a sharper torture, if he may
but assert the truth.

Job maintains his calm dignity till three of his
friends come to console him. After uttering their
lamentations over the sufferer, they sit in silence for
seven days with him, for when grief is so crushing
what can sympathy do but be silent ? Unmanned
at last, Job breaks the stillness with a bitter complaint,

cursing the day of his birth, and longing that he
may die. This leads on to a dialogue between
himself and the friends. They firmly hold that
great suffering is to be explained by great sinfulness,
and since Job's consciousness of integrity is incom-
municable, it is natural that they should sacrifice
their friend to their theology. They deal gently with
him at the first, but with each cycle of speeches the
debate grows more and more embittered. The
speeches of the friends have little significance for
our problem. They start from the assumption that
omnipotence must be righteous. Perishable man
cannot be just before God. Not only is He the
Almighty Creator, in whose sight the loftiest creatures
are unclean, but He is the All-Wise, whose ways
baffle the keenest scrutiny of man. What He does
must be right ; the Almighty cannot pervert justice.
Why, indeed, should He ? since He is too great for
man's righteousness to be any pleasure or gain to
Him. Much of the friend's speeches consists of
descriptions of God's judgements on the wicked.
To Job himself they try to be considerate, though
as the debate proceeds the strain on their forbearance
becomes increasingly severe. Eliphaz comforts Job
by reminding him how blessed is the man whom
God chastens. Yet all are convinced that the facts
point to Job's sin as the cause of his suffering, hence
they urge him to turn to God, and generally bring
their speeches to an end with a glowering picture of
the happiness that will then round off his days.
And while they also dwell on the fate of the godless,
to make good their argument and point a moral for
Job, yet their treatment of him, though it varies
with different speakers, is as tender as we could

have expected, with their theological presuppositions. Essentially the standpoint in the speeches of Elihu is identical with that of the friends. These speeches do not belong to the original work.

It is not their accusations that provoke the anger of Job so much as their vacant platitudes, their superficial maxims, their sorry attempts to solve new problems by obsolete methods, their blind pedantic orthodoxy. Surely, were they not bemused with a theology out of touch with life, they would catch the ring of sincerity in his voice, and brush aside the unworthy thought of secret sin adequate to so terrible a punishment. Their arguments fill him with scorn and irritation, but their unkindness wounds him to the quick. He had counted on their sympathy, but had been disappointed, as caravans perish from thirst, since the streams they had reckoned on are dry. At times he even appeals to their pity: 'Have pity upon me, have pity upon me, O ye my friends ; For the hand of God hath touched me.' But more often he crumples them with his scorn, and renews his contention with God.

It is in his debate with God that the interest of Job's speeches is most intense. He charges God, sometimes in language of tremendous realism, with inflicting his intolerable pains. His are the poisoned arrows that have consumed his strength. It is God who assails him like a giant, and dashes him in pieces; God who cruelly persecutes him, breaks him with a tempest and dissolves him in the storm. It is God's terrors that dismay him, His presence that troubles him, the horrible dreams which He sends that affright him. So with the Almighty for his enemy,

he is driven to bay, and turns on God with the
plain speech of the desperate :

> Therefore I will not refrain my mouth ;
> I will speak in the anguish of my spirit ;
> I will complain in the bitterness of my soul (7^{11}).

> My soul is weary of my life ;
> I will give free course to my complaint ;
> I will speak in the bitterness of my soul (10^1).

> Hold your peace, let me alone, that I may speak,
> And let come on me what will (13^{13}).

The friends have made eloquent speeches about
the might and majesty of God, His inscrutable
wisdom and the mystery of His ways. But Job is
well aware of it all, nay he himself does not lag
behind the friends in his descriptions of it. But
this only makes matters worse. There can be no
immorality like that of omnipotence and omniscience
uncontrolled by goodness. Such Job feels to be the
Immorality who governs the universe.

> Perfect and wicked He destroys.
> If the scourge slay suddenly
> At the trial of the innocent He mocks.
> The earth is given into the hand of the wicked,
> The faces of its judges He covereth ;
> If not, then who is it ? (9^{22-4}).

Of the prosperity of the wicked, Job cites

man, there is no violence in his hands and his prayer
is pure. He is sure that God knows that he is not
wicked, and though He has determined to slay him,
he will maintain his ways before Him. His righteousness he holds fast and will not let it go. This
consciousness finds its noblest expression in Job's
great defence of his past life, which perhaps touches
the loftiest point of Old Testament ethics. Sure of
himself and the justice of his cause, he brings his
self-vindication to its close with a challenge to
Yahweh that He should answer him, and the proud
declaration that as prince he would draw near to
God, bearing the indictment which his adversary
had written.

Yet the poet has wonderfully shown us the clashing
currents in Job's breast by the strange incoherence
of his language about God. He is torn between the
bitter present, and the happy memory, between the
God who is torturing him, and the God of whose
goodness he had drunk so deeply in the past. And
side by side with all his incisive complaints of God's
cruelty, and scorn of His malignant pettiness, side by
side even with the firm assertion of His immorality,
stand other utterances which recognize His righteousness. He bases the confidence he expresses in one
of his less gloomy moments, on the conviction that
a godless man shall not come before Him. He warns
the friends that God will not suffer Himself to be
flattered by lies. It is therefore natural that
appeal should alternate with invective. The appeal
is in some cases, indeed, rather remonstrance. Why
had God suffered him to be born? Why does He
contend with him, why hide His face? What are
the sins God has to bring against him? Is it good

for Him to despise His own work, or, when He has lavished so much care on fashioning His servant, wantonly destroy him? But the tone of remonstrance is softened into the tone of pathetic appeal. Would that he knew where he might find Him, that he might lay bare his case or utter his supplication. From the injustice of man he turns to God in the moving words : ' My friends scorn me, but my eye pours out tears unto God.' If he could only come face to face with God, He would not contend with him in the greatness of His power, but would give heed to his plea. He appeals to God to relax His incessant watchfulness, and give him a respite from his pain. Would that He might hide him in Sheol, keep him in secret till His Wrath were past. Here the poet advances to one of his deepest thoughts. Not only does Job appeal from man to God, but he appeals from God to God. There seems to be an irrational element in his thought. Job asks God to save him from God's wrath, to place him out of its reach, till it has spent itself. He appeals to God against God, as if God had a higher and lower self. Behind the wrathful he catches a glimpse of the gracious God. There is no umpire between them, but would not God Himself give security to God for Job? So he wins, if he cannot hold fast, the conviction, that his witness is in heaven, and He that vouches for him is on high. This reaches its climax in the famous passage 19^{25-7}, in which Job expresses his conviction that his vindicator lives, and that his innocence will at last be established. And though he does not look forward to a vindication in his lifetime, yet he believes that he will be permitted to know that his character is cleared. Not that he explain to Job why he suffers. There is no comfort offered him, but what seems like a brutal mockery. Yet if we look more closely we shall see that the speeches of Yahweh are not mere irrelevant irony. Job has taken on himself to criticize the government of the universe. But has he ever realized what the universe is, or how complex the problem of its control ? So God brings before him its wonderful phenomena in language of surpassing beauty. The mighty work of its creation, the curbing of the rebellious sea, the land of the dead, the home of light and of darkness, the ordered march of the constellations, the treasuries of snow and hail, which God has stored to overwhelm His enemies ; the frost that binds the streams, or the rain that quenches the desert's thirst, all pass before Job's mind and all are too vast, too obscure, for him to comprehend. Then God sketches a series of swift pictures of His animal creation of whose secrets Job is profoundly ignorant. Thus He brings home to him the limitation of his outlook, thus Job comes to learn the wide range of God's interests. And as we reflect more deeply we see a relevance in the Divine speeches that at first we are apt to miss. Job's language had not stopped short of blasphemy, and though he pleaded that his friends must not take too seriously the words of a desperate man, yet he deserved a sharp lesson to cure his presumption. True, he had freely confessed God's might and wisdom, he had beforehand said that God would not contend with him in the greatness of His power. But he needed to have the detail bitten into his imagination, that the vague generality might become vivid and concrete. For much of the mischief with Job lay in his self-absorption. He dwells on God's immoral control of the lot of man, but even more specially on God's immoral treatment of himself. God bids the self-centred sufferer look away at the wide universe, then he will come to a juster estimate of man's place. But even if he looks at the sentient life of the world, he will realize that man is only one among many of the objects of God's concern. All those glorious pictures of the animal creation that God flashes before his eyes are meant to show him that man's importance may easily be overrated. Especially is this the case with those unsubdued denizens of the wilderness, who live their life wholly independent of man. There, too, God sends the fertilizing shower, causing it ' to rain on a land where no man is '.

When Job confesses that he has sinned in speaking of things too wonderful for him, and with self-abhorrence repents in dust and ashes, the question arises whether we are to see in this a verification of his dread that the terror of God's majesty and His insoluble questions would force him into self-condemnation. It would be to miss the deepest teaching the poet has to give us were we to think so. By confronting him with Nature, God has taken him out of himself and convinced him of his relative insignificance. Yet even that is not the chief thing. It is no accident that the poet refrains from putting in God's mouth any explanation of Job's sufferings. To men oppressed by the mystery of their own or the world's pain, the explanation of an individual case is of little worth, unless it admits of wider application. And for Job himself the explanation is unneeded.   He has received a new experience :

> I had heard of Thee by the hearing of the ear ;
> But now mine eye seeth Thee,
> Wherefore I abhor myself, and repent
> In dust and ashes (42^{5-6}).

It is the vision of God which has released him from his problem.   His suffering is as mysterious as ever, but plain or mysterious, why should it vex him any longer ?   He has seen God and has entered into rest.   The only answer we can get to the problem of pain is, the poet would tell us, this answer.   The soul's certainty is the soul's secret. The spirit has escaped its difficulties by soaring above them.   If we know God, no other knowledge matters.   For ourselves we have won our way to unspeakable peace.   As we dwell in the secret place of the Most High and abide under the shadow of the Almighty, we see the universe from a new point of view.   We can give no answer to its questions, no solution of its baffling riddles.   But since we know God we can trust Him to the uttermost ;   we know, incredible though it may seem, that the world's misery does not contradict the love of God.   It was therefore with deliberate intent that the poet put in God's lips no hint of the reason of Job's suffering. To trust God when we understand Him would be but a sorry triumph for religion.   To trust God when we have every reason for distrusting Him, save our inward certainty of Him, is the supreme victory of religion.   This is the victory which Job achieves.   But he can achieve it only as God takes the initiative and gives him the revelation of Himself.

Yet God by the very action He took at the Satan's instigation, placed not Job only, but Himself on His trial. If the Satan is to be convinced that Job's piety is disinterested, it must be through the tests that he imposes. For God to accept the challenge meant that He accepted a grave responsibility. Job has to be the involuntary subject of this experiment, he must suffer that God's confidence may be justified. To some at any rate this will not seem a complete vindication of God's action, it, too, must go with other partially-solved mysteries. The difficulty would probably be less to a Semite than to ourselves. Yet the author felt it, and for that reason added or retained the Epilogue. It is not that Job needed his restoration in order to regain his confidence in ᵍod. Had he been doomed to end his days in pain, he could walk through the valley in the memory of the vision of God. But then the reader would have been very unfavourably impressed by God's treatment of him. Now he feels that God has made amends to His loyal servant for the pain He has made him endure. To estimate the Epilogue aright we must not forget that the author had to keep the treatment of his subject within the limits of the earthly life, and could not work with the conception of a happy immortality. And we must remember that the compensation given to Job is to clear God's character, not in any way to reaffirm the old theory that the righteous must be fortunate.

What lessons then has the book for ourselves ? It bids us in the first place be resolute in facing the facts. To flatter God by timidly denying their existence, is to do Him no service, but only to draw down His anger (13^{7-11}, 42^{7-8}). To smother them is

to leave doubt lurking unquietly in the heart, to
recognize them may be the path to peace. The
next lesson is that we cannot argue for the invariable
connexion of sin and suffering, or of righteousness
and prosperity. We ought, on the contrary, to be
prepared to find in many cases that the wicked
prosper, while the righteous are doomed to pain.
Further, suffering may be sent to test the reality of
our piety, and its freedom from the vice of self-
interest. Once more we are bidden to remember
that man is not the exclusive object of God's regard,
and that he is just one member of a very complex
organism. It is given him to see only a small section
of the universe, he cannot pass judgement on the
whole from his knowledge of so tiny a part. The
most important lesson is that even though no specu-
lative solution be possible to us, we may so know
God as to be sure of His love, and be content to
suffer without understanding or caring to understand the reason. Such an attitude is not one of
resignation or aquiescence, but of glad acceptance,
because we are assured of the love that sends the
sorrow. There is, moreover, one very important
contribution which the poet does not make, but
which I am inclined to think, he meant to suggest.
He could not work confidently with the conception
of immortality. But he was clearly tempted by it,
and seems to look for light from it. Let it be noticed
in what gloomy colours he paints Sheol. From it
there is no return, it is a land of darkness and the
shadow of death, of darkness so dense that its very
light is as darkness. While the tree may be cut down
and yet bud at the scent of water, man is never
wakened from the sleep of death. Job's words are

so strong that it is hard to suppress the feeling that the poet intended to force revulsion. And the thought of a return to life is definitely before him. Probably he can do no more than turn wistfully toward it, feeling it almost too good to be true. It may seem strange that no reference is made to the vicarious character of suffering, if, as I have assumed, the poem is later than the Servant passages in the Book of Isaiah. Probably we should account for this by the fact that the author of the latter was dealing with the sufferings of the nation, whereas the author of Job was concerned with the problem of individual suffering.

CHAPTER SIX

Songs in the Night

IT is no part of my plan to discuss those passages in the Old Testament that connect the suffering, of which they speak, with the sin of the sufferer. Under this head a large number of passages in the Psalter falls. Yet there are many which treat the suffering endured by the community, the godly, or the individual Psalmist as a mystery. They are cries out of the depths, their constant burden is ' How long ? ' It is not necessary, however, to do much more than give a brief summary, since for the most part the writers do not get beyond complaint and the prayer for deliverance. Little short of half the Psalms contain mournful appeals to God for salvation from pain or oppression. It is often far from clear whether it is an individual or the community that is speaking, and the historical conditions which the Psalms presuppose are frequently known to us only in the most general way. In some cases it is a heathen enemy which is trampling on Israel, in other cases it is the lax, irreligious Jews who oppress their pious countrymen, in others the individual writer who suffers at the hands of some enemy. With the despair and self-pity there are mingled bitter curses on the oppressor. We may palliate them by the consideration that the Psalmists identified their cause with the cause of God, and by assuming that often the community and not an individual is the sufferer. But it is one of the numerous signs in the religion of

Israel, how much there was needed the coming of One who should pray, 'Father, forgive them, for they know not what they do'. The causes of their affliction, apart from their own sin, are variously enumerated. It may be the sins of their forefathers, as in Psalm 79[8]: 'Remember not against us the sins of our ancestors.' It may be Yahweh's anger, for which no motive can be assigned, the anger itself being simply inferred from the consequences it has involved. Or again, it may be Yahweh's indifference. He has cast off His people. Thus in the dark days of dishonour and defeat, when God no longer went forth with the Jewish hosts, and made His people a derision to the heathen, it is not in their own sin that they find the reason, for they have not forgotten God, or dealt falsely in His covenant. So far from that, it is their very loyalty to God, which has brought disaster upon them :

Nay, but for Thy sake are we killed all the day long,
We are counted as sheep for the slaughter (Psalm 44[22]).

It can only be that God has lapsed into forgetfulness of His people. He is as one who sleeps, unconscious of the tragedy that He ought to stay. Hence the Psalmist seeks to stir Him from His sluggish indolence with the impassioned cry :

Rouse thyself ! Why sleepest thou, O Lord ?
Awake, cast us not off for ever.

In Psalm 92[6] we have an interesting passage probably referring to some recent event, in which it is said to be a mystery unknown to the senseless, that it is part of God's plan for the wicked to flourish in order that they might be destroyed. Twice we have remarkable references to ' the gods' as responsible for the wrongs that are rampant on earth. To these ' Elohim ' Yahweh, according to Deuteronomy 32[8], had allotted the heathen nations, while He retained Israel as His own portion. They are identical with ' the host of the high ones on high ' of whom we read in Isaiah 24[21], and with the angel princes in the Book of Daniel. Like the angels of the churches in the Revelation, they are held responsible for the actions of those committed to them. The situation in Psalms 58 and 82, is one of misery for Israel caused by the violence of the heathen. For this violence the heavenly patrons are held guilty, so when, as in Job, they come to present themselves before Yahweh, He reproves them for the injustice of their rule, and threatens them with the punishment of death :

> I said, Ye are gods ;
> And all of you sons of the Most High.
> Howbeit, ye shall die like men,
> And fall like one of the princes (Psalm 82[6]).

There are three Psalms which deal specifically with our problem, Psalms 37, 49, and 73. The first of these is an alphabetical Psalm, and we are therefore prepared to find considerable repetition, and no strict development of the thought. The author rebukes complaints against God on account of the prosperity of the wicked, and bids his readers be not envious of them. Rather let them wait patiently on Yahweh, for if they delight in Him He will give them their heart's desire and make their righteousness go forth as the light. Vexation at the success of the godless leads only to evil doing. Why indeed should they nourish vexation ? The wicked plot the death of the righteous, but Yahweh mocks, for it is their own death that is coming. Soon the judgement is to burst, when they will be rooted out of the land and vanish like smoke. Those who are cursed of Him shall be cut off. But the humble, who wait on Yahweh, shall inherit the land for ever, and have delight in abundance of peace. Better then to have little like the righteous rather than the wealth of the wicked. And even under present conditions the righteous man and his children do not come to want. Moreover, even before the judgement on the wicked comes, examples are to be seen of the unrighteous flourishing like the cedars of Lebanon, but suddenly cut off. Probably there is no reference to the after life in verses 37-8, though it is uncertain whether the meaning is that there is a posterity or a future to the man of peace, but not to the wicked. The Psalm would have been in place in the Book of Proverbs ; it is deservedly a favourite for devotional reading, but it does not advance the solution of the problem.

Psalm 49 is much more striking. The author propounds the question why he should fear in time of calamity, when the wealthy seek to overthrow him. No man can ransom himself[a] from Sheol, or secure for himself an earthly immortality. Wise

---

[a] The text reads, ' No man can by any means ransom a brother '. But ' ransom himself ' is the sense required. The word for ' brother ', *āch*, is also placed in a strange position at the beginning of the sentence. We should read *ak*, ' surely ', or ' but'.

and fool die alike.   The grave[b] is their house for ever
and man perishes like the beasts.   Death drives the
self-confident down to Sheol, as a shepherd drives
his flock, while the upright rule over them in the
morning.[c]   But the Psalmist expresses the confidence
that God will ransom him from Sheol and take him.
Therefore there is no need for fear when a man
grows rich, for at death he must leave his riches
behind him.

Here the author does not appeal, as the author of
Psalm 37, to an imminent catastrophe, but to
life's normal issue.   All die, and no man will ever
be so rich as to bribe God to release him from the
universal fate.   But is a commonplace of this
kind worthy of the introduction, in which the author
invites all nations to listen to his wise utterances ?
Hardly, even if we emphasize the fact that the
possession of wealth makes death harder than it is
for those who have little or nothing to leave.   It is

[b] The text reads *qirbām*, ' their inward part'. But this yields no
proper sense, ' their inward part their houses for ever'.   We should
read with the LXX, Syriac, Vulgate, and Targum, *qibrām*, ' their
grave', or perhaps better still point *qebarīm*, ' graves'.

[c] The sense is not at all clear. ' In the morning ' rather takes us
into Apocalyptic ; when the great world-judgement breaks, then the
upright will rule over the wicked.   But it scarcely seems suitable
here, for the author does not operate with this conception, and he is
speaking of what happens to the wicked after death.   Wellhausen
strikes out the clause ' and the upright rule over them'.   He says it
' is an interpolation which is extremely inappropriate in this passage.
It shows, however, most characteristically the longing of the Jews
for Messianic rule.'   He retains the word translated ' in the morning',
babbōqer, but translates ' soon ' connecting with the next clause.
Klostermann retains the consonants, but points and divides
differently, reading *weyēredū bemēyshārīm*, ' and they go down
smoothly ' or ' by level ways'.   This connects very well with the
preceding words, though whether it is quite what would have been
expected is more dubious.   Duhm accepts it.

therefore probable that we should seek the wisdom he is uttering in verse 15. There he expresses the confidence that God will ransom him from the hand of Sheol, ' for He will take me'. Frequently this is thought to mean no more than that Yahweh will deliver him from premature death. The hand of Sheol is ready to clutch him as its prey, but Yahweh plucks him out of its reach. In that case the meaning would be that while he has to die in due course, he is saved from imminent death. But the context shows that here we ought to have a contrast between the fate of the Psalmist and that of the ungodly rich. We should have a contrast if the latter were said to die prematurely. But this is not the case. They die in the normal course of things in spite of their wealth. The contrast lies between what the wicked cannot buy from God, and what the Psalmist receives from God as an act of grace. Such a contrast would be given if the writer said that while the wicked died, he lived on upon earth. But that is not the contrast he has in mind. All must die, he as well as the rest. But while the wicked are driven down to the dim under-world, God saves him when he dies, from this fate, and takes him to live with Himself. The phraseology recalls the story of Enoch, and we must reckon the Psalm as one of the immortality Psalms. This new doctrine it is which is regarded by the author as a wise saying, worthy the world's attention.

The Seventy-third Psalm strikes a still deeper note. It opens with a confession of God's goodness to the pure in heart, which springs from the experience the Psalmist is going to describe. For this conviction had not been reached without a hard struggle, in which

H

For I was envious at the boasters,
When I saw the success of the wicked.
For they have no pangs,[e]
Sound and fat is their body.
In the misery of mortals they have no part,
And with other men they are not stricken.
Therefore pride is their necklace,
A garment of violence covers them.
Their iniquity[f] comes forth out of fatness,
The imaginations of their heart overflow.
They mock and speak in wickedness,
Perversity[g] they speak from on high.
They have set their mouth in the heavens,
And their tongue walks in the earth,
Therefore the people return to them,
And they find no blemish in them ;[h]

[e] Instead of *l*emōthām, 'at their death', we should no doubt, dividing the consonants, read lāmō tām. The former word means ' to them ' (' there are no pangs to them '), the latter word is that translated ' sound '.

[f] Reading with the LXX and most commentators ' aw ōnāmō instead of the text, ' ēynēmō, ' their eye '. The meaning is that their iniquity comes ' out of a gross, unfeeling heart' (Driver, *Parallel Psalter*, page 208).

[g] So, rather than as ' oppression', Buhl in the last edition of Gesenius' *Hebrew Lexicon*, and Duhm.

[h] The Hebrew margin reads: ' Therefore his people return hither, and waters of fullness are drained by them', and this is supported by the versions against the Kethib, ' he bringeth back his people hither'. The text is suspicious. Wellhausen, improving on Lagarde's emendation, reads for the first line, ' Therefore are they satisfied with bread ', which involves little alteration, and gives an excellent parallel to the second line. Baethgen feels that bread and water is not what we should expect in a description of the fortunes of the wealthy oppressor. He thinks with several that the reference to water is figurative for the false teaching of the wicked, which is drunk in by their fellow-countrymen. Accordingly he does not emend the text. The translation given above follows Duhm's reading, 'ām 'ăleyhem in the first line, and mūm lō yimts'eū in the second, which is little more than a fresh division of the consonants. The meaning is that the people judge from the prosperity of the wicked that they have chosen the better part.

And they say,[i] ' How does God know,
And is their knowledge in the Most High ? '
See, these are the wicked,
And, at ease for ever, they increase their power.
' Surely in vain have I cleansed my heart,
And washed in innocency my hands ;
Yet I was stricken all the day,
And my reproof came every morning.'
I said, ' Thus will I speak ';[j]
Lo, to the generation of thy sons was I traitor.
And I pondered how to know this,
Misery was in it in mine eyes,
Till I penetrated into God's holy secrets,[k]
Considered their destiny.
Surely thou settest them in slippery places,
Castest them down into ruins.
How are they become a desolation in a moment,
Hurried away, ended by terrors.

[i] Apparently it is the people mentioned in the previous verse, who are the speakers. Opinions differ as to where their speech ends. I think, on the whole, it is best to make it embrace this verse only, the poet himself resuming with ' See these are the wicked '.

[j] The present text is incomplete, ' If I said I will tell like,' we need to complete it with ' this ' or ' these things '. I follow Baethgen in striking out ' if ', which may have arisen through dittography of the next two letters. The poet *had* spoken in this way.

[k] The line is commonly translated, 'Until I went into the sanctuary of God '. Had he then been staying away all the time his trouble was vexing him ? The word is plural, ' sanctuaries ', and it yields a much finer thought if, with Hitzig and some other scholars, we take the word to mean God's sacred mysteries. There is no need to infer with Duhm that the poet was actually initiated into mysteries, which gave instruction on the life after death. At the same time I agree with him in thinking that in what follows we have a description of the fate of the oppressor after death. Experience would have contradicted, for so profound a thinker, any such view of their fate as happening in this life.

As a dream after waking shall they be,[l]
When thou art aroused, thou shalt despise their
  semblance.
When my heart was soured,
And I felt a stab in my reins,
Then I was a brute and knew not,
A very beast[m] I became toward Thee.
But I am continually with Thee,
Thou holdest my right hand,
With Thy counsel Thou wilt guide me,
And afterwards to glory Thou wilt take me,[n]

[l] The present text suggests that when God awakes He will despise
their semblance, as a man despises his dream when he wakes from it
to realities.   The thought, however, that God is at present asleep and
the victim of an illusion which He will despise when He awakes
cannot have been in the Psalmist's mind.   We shall accordingly be
obliged to fall back on the interpretation that when God rouses
Himself to judgement He despises their semblance, just as a man
despises His dream when He wakes from it.   This, however, is
not the immediate impression of the simile.   Wellhausen strikes
out 'ădōnāy, ' O Lord '.   He gives no reason, but it may be supposed
was influenced by some such consideration as that mentioned
above.   The sense we want seems to be that when a man is wakened
from the ignorance in which he now slumbers, he will see things as
they are, and despise the phantoms which now seem such solid
realities.   This is the sense given in the translation above.   Instead
of striking out 'ădōnāy we may suppose with Duhm that it is
substituted for Yahweh, as it was usually substituted in reading.
If we further correct Yahweh into yiheyu we get the sense, ' shall
they be '.   We have a similar case probably in the famous passage
Psalm 45[6], where 'ĕlōhīm should probably be yiheyeh, ' Thy throne
shall be for ever and ever '.

[m] So Driver translates, taking behēmōth as an intensive plural. Some
think behemoth is intended, as in Job. Duhm reads the singular.

[n] I take achar as an adverb meaning afterwards, and kābōd as
accusative expressing direction, ' to glory '.   We might also
translate ' with glory '.   The Hebrew is no doubt peculiar ; Wellhausen thinks it indefensible and reads achăreyka beyād, ' And
takest me by the hand after Thee ' (see also Smend, Alttestamentliche
Religionsgeschichte, First Edition, p. 453). The alteration yields a
fine thought, but it is one already substantially expressed, and one
not nearly so deep as that given by the present text.   If accepted,
it would be better to read beyādī. Cheyne (Jewish Religious Life,
page 240) reads : ' And make known to me the path of glory.'

Whom have I in heaven ?
And possessing Thee I delight in nought upon earth.
Though my flesh and my heart fail away,
God is for ever the rock of my heart and my portion.
For, lo, they that go far from Thee shall perish,
Thou dost cut off every one that goes wantonly astray
    from Thee.
But as for me, nearness to God is my good,
I have made my refuge in the Lord Yahweh,
To recount all Thy works.[o]

If the Psalm has been correctly interpreted, the
solution of the problem is attained by reference to
the state after death.   In this it differs from Psalm
37, which also solves the difficulty by eschatology,
but simply with a reference to the judgement in
which the wicked are to be slain, while the righteous
survive and inherit the land.   It moves essentially
on the same lines as that of Psalm 49, but it heightens
the contrast, and is incomparably richer and deeper
in expression.   How striking is the difference
between the bloodless description of the one and the
lurid terrors of the other !   And how tame the
utterance of hope for a happy future compared with
the wonderful picture of the soul in deep, untroubled
fellowship with God, so deep that Death cannot sever
it, so perfect that heaven itself can add nothing to it !
Here also the writer has really reached a point
where his problem sinks into insignificance.   He lives
in God and in that rapture the pains of earth sting

_____

[o] Duhm may be right in thinking that this line is a later addition.
The impression of the Psalm is not strengthened by it, and its
regularity is disturbed since the line has no parallel.

him no longer.   Since God is his portion, the sufferings of this life do not disturb his peace.   And even the glory, to which he knows that he will be taken, means essentially nothing more than he has already in his possession of God.   Nowhere else in the Old Testament is the essence of religion set forth with such power and such beauty, no passage makes so deep an appeal to our inmost heart.   It ranks with Jeremiah's prophecy of the New Covenant, with the Second Isaiah's description of the Suffering Servant, with the fourth chapter of the Book of Jonah, those most marvellous monuments of the religious genius of Israel.

CHAPTER SEVEN

The Apocalyptist and the Pessimist

THE miseries, which filled the century after the Return, lived on through long stretches of the centuries that followed, relieved by happier intervals, and culminating in the horrors and splendours of the Maccabean age. Our Psalter reflects the condition of things during the post-exilic period, though it may include some poems of an earlier time. But other currents were set in motion or accelerated by the sufferings of Judah, which demand some notice before the discussion draws to its close.

The sorrows of the present sent many for comfort to the future. It must be, so the pious thought in many an agonizing moment, when ground by the heel of the foreign tyrant or of their own apostate countrymen, it must surely be that day cannot but dawn after darkness so intense. How could life otherwise be tolerable, if when endurance was strained to snapping point, the hope of imminent deliverance did not lift them above their despair? So they fed their courage with the illusion that they were living at the thrilling hour of crisis. As they flagged in the dreary march they said to each other, God's kingdom will break on our sight at the next turn of the road. They studied the ancient prophets, combined their pictures of the glorious future into a systematic whole, and sought from their scattered hints to formulate a prophetic chronology. Loss of political independence led to the expectation of deliverance by catastrophe rather than by an evolution from the existing political situation. As the drama reaches its climax God strikes in and crushes the heathen oppressor. In an instant, without preparation, the transition is effected from dense gloom to the radiant light. The strange symbolism and elaborate allegories are a development of features found in the prophets, the later prophets especially, and perhaps were also fostered by the need for caution in perilous times. The seer wrapped up in an allegory what it was unsafe to utter without disguise. These apocalypses were as a rule represented as revelations to some ancient seer. They often sketch the history from the assumed author's date to the time of the real author, events that have already happened being described with great circumstantiality, which gives place to vague generalities when history in the guise of prediction passes into prediction proper. There is usually a more or less elaborate angelology.

Of apocalypses in the strict sense of the term we have only one in the Old Testament, the Book of Daniel. But some earlier prophecies have a strong apocalyptic colouring. Zephaniah, though in a mild degree, is perhaps our earliest example, but in Ezekiel it is very marked. Zechariah, Joel, and especially Isaiah 24-7 also show us prophecy moving toward apocalyptic.

Joel, whose date may most plausibly be fixed in the fourth century B.C., speaks in a time of great distress, caused partly by drought, which has dried up the streams and given rise to bush and forest fires, but chiefly by an exceptionally severe plague of locusts. The description of the locusts is that of a poet, not of a naturalist, and any exaggeration must be thus explained. The locusts are not a metaphor for soldiers, nor are they supernatural, demoniacal locusts, like those in the Book of Revelation. They are ordinary locusts, but since the prophet sees in them the harbingers of the Day of Yahweh, an eschatological hue is reflected back upon them. So terrible has been the devastation, that the daily meal and drink offering at the Temple have had to be suspended, an ominous portent to the feeling of antiquity, since it seemed to snap the link which bound Yahweh to His people. The prophet calls for a fast and for mourning, bids his countrymen rend their hearts and not their garments and turn to Yahweh. Yet, unlike the early prophets, he complains of no specific sins, so that we may reasonably conclude that he inferred from Judah's calamity its sinfulness in God's sight. And this is confirmed by the fact that the trouble was healed by a solemn assembly, not by moral reformation and the forsaking of definite sins. In that case our problem is conceived really on conventional lines. The severe suffering of Judah is due to its sin, though what this sin may be is not known, and its existence is a mere inference from the extreme distress under which the country is labouring.

It is not necessary for our purpose to discuss at length the apocalypse which we now read in Isaiah 24–7. Although Duhm's argument, accepted by Cheyne, Marti, and apparently Skinner, for its composite character, and his analysis, seem to me in the main convincing, I cannot accept the second and first-century dates, which he assigns to it. The period from Artaxerxes Ochus to Alexander the Great appears to offer the most suitable occasion, and most worthily to explain the language employed. The problem of Judah's suffering emerges only slightly, though it lies behind much that the writers say. The main apocalypse describes a universal judgement on the nations for bloodshed and oppression. The chief insertion is 26^{1-19}, which begins with praise for God's mercies, and passes into desire for complete deliverance, ending with the anticipation of a resurrection to fill the depleted land. Perhaps 27^{7-11} is another insertion, a passage unhappily very obscure, but apparently tracing Judah's present evil condition to its sin, finding encouragement in the mildness of God's earlier judgements, and promising pardon upon repentance. The points that specially demand attention are the reference to ' the host of the height on high ' (24^{21}), and the prediction of the annihilation of death (25^8), and of a resurrection (26^{19}). The first of these touches a point already mentioned. The author glancing over the blood-stained history of the great empires, and foretelling their punishment through the mighty political convulsions that are about to desolate the world, includes not simply the earthly, but also the heavenly rulers of the nations, in the punishment Yahweh is about to inflict. Here we have the same thought as in Psalms 58 and 82, that the miseries of the world are largely to be accounted for by the misgovernment of the angelic guardians of the nations, who are here represented as in Psalm 82, as doomed to punishment, though the form of the penalty differs. The reference to the annihilation of death does not arise in connexion with our problem, and I refer to it here simply for its relation to eschatological questions which do arise at some points of our inquiry. The prediction of a resurrection is important, since it is the earliest instance of the transference to the individual of the hope that had previously been expressed for the nation. It is quite easy to see how this took place. The writer is troubled that the land is so thinly peopled, and rises to the great conviction that God's life-giving dew shall fall on those who sleep in the dust, and cause them to arise, so that the land may once more be thickly inhabited. It is only of pious Israelites (' thy dead ') that the author is thinking.

It would be hard to overrate the influence of the Book of Daniel on later religious thought. It was issued about 165 B.C. to encourage the Jews in the terrible persecution they were suffering from Antiochus Epiphanes for loyalty to their religion. Much of it has no direct bearing on our problem, except in so far as it is designed to assure the faithful Jews that the oppressor shall soon be broken and the reign of the saints begin. Two special points must be noticed since they do bear on the special question before us. Both are developments of what we have found in Isaiah 24–7. One is the place assigned to the angelic princes. The angel who appears to Daniel in the tenth chapter explains the delay in his arrival by saying that for twenty-one days the prince of Persia had withstood him, but ' Michael, one of the chief princes ', came to help him. He informs him further that as soon as he has revealed the message, he must return to fight with the prince of Persia, and afterwards with the prince of Greece. In this conflict ' there is none that strengtheneth

himself with me against these, except Michael your
prince '. Toward the close of the vision it is said
that when Antiochus falls: 'Michael shall stand up,
the great prince who stands for the children of thy
people ' (12^1). There is to be an unprecedented
tribulation, but all who are written in the book, i.e.,
the book of life, shall be delivered. Here, once more,
the miseries of earth are due to the angelic powers.
The conflicts of earth have first been fought in
heaven between the patron angels of the nations.
While in Deuteronomy the other nations have each
its angel, but Israel has Yahweh, in Daniel Israel
has Michael for its angel. This development is
largely due to the overwhelming sense of the
transcendence of God.

The second point is the prediction of a resurrection
'And many that sleep in the dust of the earth
shall awake, some to everlasting life, and some to
reproaches and everlasting abhorrence. And they
that be wise shall shine as the brightness of the
firmament, and they that turn many to righteousness
as the stars for ever and ever ' (12^{2-3}). The passage
springs out of the historical circumstances. The
hope of a life with God in heaven had already found
expression, and a physical resurrection had been
predicted as the remedy for the depopulation of
the land. But what works specially on our author's
mind is the heroic constancy to God displayed
by the martyrs. When Israel triumphs, and God's
kingdom is set up on earth, they must be raised
from the dead to share in its glories. The wise,
who turn many to righteousness, are apparently
distinguished from the rank and file of the risen ones.
But the passage reflects also the internal conflicts

in the contemporary Judaism. The apostates who have renounced the faith of their people are not to remain in Sheol. They are brought back to life, that there in the Messianic kingdom they may for ever hear the reproaches and endure the loathing of those whom they have betrayed.

Not all Jews could take refuge from the miseries of the present in glowing pictures of an imminent golden age. Where faith has lost its spring, the earnest soul, that is keenly sensitive to the miseries of mankind, drifts easily toward pessimism. Such was the case of him to whom we owe the Book of Ecclesiastes.[a] Its date is not certain, but we may

---

[a] For a statement of the critical conclusions that are here pre-supposed, I may refer to my article ' Ecclesiastes ' in Hastings' *Dictionary of the Bible*. Since that was written other theories have been advanced. The most important is perhaps Siegfried's in his commentary on the work in Nowack's *Hand-Kommentar* (1898). It reminds one to some extent of his treatment of ' Job ' in *The Sacred Books of the Old Testament*. The original author was a pessimist, who had broken with Judaism, and was mainly influenced by Stoicism. His work was glossed by four writers representing Epicurean Sadduceeism, Jewish wisdom, Jewish piety, and a prudential view of life. After a first redactor had compiled the work and added 12^8 as a closing formula, 12^{9-10} was added, then 12^{11-12}, and 12^{13-14} by the final redactor. The English reader may see an outline of the theory and a brief sketch of the contents of the book from this point of view in Siegfried's article ' Wisdom ' in Hastings' *Dictionary of the Bible*. Its value lies in its forcing into prominence the different tendencies that are present in the book : but I think more of them could be combined in a single personality than Siegfried admits. His theory is accepted by H. P. Smith (*Old Testament History*, p. 439), but is adversely criticized by Laue in a monograph entitled *Das Buch Koheleth und die Interpolationshypothese Siegfried's* (Wittenburg, 1900). Other discussions are to be found in Cheyne (*Jewish Religious Life*, pp. 183-208 ; Herodian date, interpolation in orthodox interest, omission of objectionable passages, deliberate dislocation of order to destroy the connexion). Davidson's article in the *Encyclopædia Biblica* reaches practically the same results as the article in Hastings' *Dictionary*. Cheyne adds a useful series of notes on recent discussions.

with most probability assign it to the close of the third or the opening of the second century B.C., though the possibility of a Hasmonean or even of a Herodian date is not excluded. The author's meaning is not always clear, and two causes have combined to conceal it still more from the general reader. One is that Solomon has been regarded as the author, and in direct antithesis to the main current of its thought has been imagined to have written it in a penitent old age. The other is that it has been interpolated in an orthodox interest, to break the point of much that the author says. Yet we need not push this just conclusion to the extreme of finding as many writers as there are tendencies in the book, for the author was a man whose thought was not rigidly consistent, and whose expression varied with his mood. In the main he has a definite view of life. This is that all is vanity. As he looks back on his own career and sums up its impression, this is the verdict he deliberately passes on it. Life is meaningless and a mockery, since man's powers crave a sphere of action, and their exercise achieves no abiding result. The fundamental law of existence is that life is a closed circle from which man cannot get away. All things move in a cycle : what is now, has been before, and will be again, and there is no new thing under the sun. Hence there can be no progress. There is no profit in our toil ; we are climbing a treadmill, not a stairway to heights yet unreached. All things are fixed in their order by God, and occur regardless of our endeavours to help or thwart them. What God does is for ever ; no human effort can increase or lessen the sum total of things. Hence all efforts for reform are hopeless, the wheel of fate spins round, and man, himself lashed to it, can neither accelerate nor retard its motion. If we imagine that anything is new, that is an error. For generations ago it was known, and it is only the fact, that those who knew it have died and their very memory is forgotten, which makes it possible for it to be thought a novelty. As the author thinks of this dreary grind, his soul is filled with loathing for its unspeakable weariness : ' All things are full of weariness ; man cannot utter it ; the eye is not satisfied with seeing nor the ear with hearing ' (1[8]).

Now the thought that there is a reign of law, a fixed cycle in which history moves, might bring inspiration to a man. If he could discover the law, then he might work with it and make himself one with the main stream of the universe ; even though his work ended in nothing permanent, he still might win a large satisfaction for his own brief life. But this is just what he cannot do. God has planned minutely the whole order of things, nay, He has implanted within men the instincts and impulses that move them to busy themselves with the things He has ordained. But it is man's misery that God has deliberately withheld knowledge, while He has imparted impulse. Hence man is driven to seek his satisfaction in the world, but he seeks it blindfold. Careful foresight may just as well lead him wrong as right. The man gifted with wisdom may think he has detected the law of events. But this is self-deception, ' though a wise man think to know it, yet he shall not be able to find it '. Thus man's utmost avails him nothing. He does not know his time, hence he may ruin everything by excessive zeal or a too prudent caution. Qualifications and ability do not serve him : ' The race is not to the swift, nor the battle to the strong, neither yet bread to the wise, nor yet riches to men of understanding, nor yet favour to men of skill ; but time and chance happeneth to them all ' (9^{11}). Hence, while to the eye of God everything comes in its order and all things are beautiful in their season, man who has no clue to the maze, can see in the world's happenings no harmonious order, but only the reign of caprice. It is mere chance whether he hits or misses the moment of fate, whether the plans he has laid so carefully coincide or not with the plans of God. Moreover, God has freely chosen to make man's life thus unmeaning. He guards His secret, resolute that men shall not divine it. He wills to humble their proud conceit, that they may know themselves to be no better than the beasts. Thus they are snared in an evil net, since the knowledge is withheld that would enable them to escape its meshes.

This hopeless view of life is not merely asserted. the author seeks to prove it. He has reached it as the result of exhaustive experiment. He had tried the roads which lead, as men think, to satisfaction. But always his search had ended in disenchantment. Wisdom he found to be vain. The very impulse to seek it involved him in sore labour, and in much wisdom he discovered much sorrow, and increase of knowledge he learnt to be increase of pain. Some advantage it is true, wisdom has over folly. Yet it all ends in death and utter oblivion, and in the long run the wise is no better than the fool. But if wisdom does not satisfy, may not happiness be attained through pleasure ? Clothing his experiences here, as in the previous case, in the form of experiences of Solomon, the writer tells us that he sought satisfaction in the delights of the senses, in vast riches, in works of building and husbandry. He was not a sensualist for the sake of wallowing in debauchery. His wisdom remained with him, in other words, he investigated pleasure as a scientific experimentalist bent on discovering the answer to a problem. And here, too, he reached an unfavourable result, and felt that he hated life for its ineffectiveness.

In the course of his book he communicates more of his observations. The labour of life is vain, since the wise man may have a fool for his heir. Moreover, if he accumulates wealth, it means the burden of a larger household ; it implies incessant toil by day, and anxious, sleepless nights ; he may lose it all and be plunged into poverty ; or he may lose the capacity to enjoy the pleasures and comforts it might procure him ; and in any case he has at last to die and relinquish it. Once more, wherever we look abroad in the world we see misery. Government is an organized system of oppression. We need not wonder, for those who oppress the subject are themselves the victims of the rapacity of their superiors, and the latter similarly suffer from those above them. Thus on the hapless subjects of a province weighs the accumulated oppression of rank above rank of civil servants. And as the author, tender-hearted but despairing, considers the tears of the wronged and how they have no comforter, he exclaims, far better the fate of those long dead than of those who suffer these intolerable pains, but best of all is it never to have been born. He had seen the enthusiasm of the people when the reign of an old

king, too old to mend his ways or take counsel,
had given place to the reign of a new monarch.   But
he knew that here too disillusion was bound to come.
He had seen the inversion of social distinctions,
slaves on horseback and princes trudging on foot,
fools in positions of dignity.   He had marked,
perhaps he had suffered from, the ubiquity of spies,
and learnt how necessary it was to avoid all criticism
of the ruling powers.   He had known great benefits
repaid with ungrateful forgetfulness, and he had
noticed how the wisdom of the poor was despised.   He
is especially bitter about women, wherein there is no
doubt disclosed a singularly unfortunate experience :
' One man out of a thousand have I found, but
a woman among all these I have not found.'

The misgovernment of the world by man is all in
a line with the government of God.   On this, however, the author speaks with different voices.   He
refers to the divine judgement, and says that it shall
be well with those who fear God.   Yet he tells us
that a righteous man perishes in his righteousness,
and a wicked man prolongs his life in evil doing.   All
have the same fate. ' All things come alike to all :
there is one event to the righteous and to the wicked ;
to the good and to the evil ; to the clean and to the
unclean ; to him that sacrificeth, and him that
sacrificeth not : as is the good so is the sinner ; and
he that sweareth as he that feareth an oath.   This
is an evil, in all that is done under the sun, that
there is one event to all '   (9^{2-3}).   The author
has not abandoned a belief in God, but the belief has
been practically emptied of religious content.   He
knows no rapture of sweet familiar intercourse, but
thinks of God as the austere ruler, who is to be

dreaded and on whose forbearance it would be perilous to presume. Into His presence man should enter with caution, and remembering that God is in heaven, while he is on earth, he should not be too glib in his religious exercises, but should see that his words are few. Especially he should beware lest he suffer himself to be carried away by religious enthusiasm and undertake pledges, which he will not wish to carry out in cold blood. ' When thou vowest a vow unto God, defer not to pay it ; for He has no pleasure in fools ' (5⁴).

The author's maxims for the conduct of life are of singular interest. At the best, life is wretched. It is better to go to the house of mourning than the house of feasting, and the day of death is better than the day of birth. It is well for man to be patient and resigned, to accept the inevitable and recognize that it is impossible to straighten what God has made crooked. While all enterprise is made uncertain by man's ignorance of God's design, yet it is best to work on, disregarding this fact. Do not, he says, wait timidly till opportunity seems more favourable, but boldly venture. Do not relax your efforts, for one may fail and another succeed, indeed, both alike may chance to prosper. Withal, it is well to be prudent and to prepare for possible mischances. A special form that prudence may wisely take is benevolence distributed over a wide area, for calamity may come, and possibly some who have been helped may be willing to repay their debt.

There is no remedy for the ills of life, but there is some mitigation. ' A man has no better thing under the sun than to eat and drink and enjoy

Old Testament a preparation for Christ. Such a preparation was not simply along the line of anticipation and approach. Rightly to appraise Christianity we required an object lesson, which should convince us how much the world needed it. The moral bankruptcy of Greece and Rome present us with an impressive example of what we are seeking. But Judaism, was it not competent to carry through the world's reformation? We cannot forget the close approximations to Christianity, which at its best, the religion of Israel achieved. But we do well to ponder also the darker side. Its legalism, its tedious casuistry, its danger of self-righteousness, its narrow exclusiveness, its bitter vindictiveness, all these must be taken into account ; while we must never forget how needful it is for us to cleanse our own religion from these faults by strenuous fidelity to the spirit and temper of the Gospel. And I think that Ecclesiastes is here peculiarly instructive. It puts the logic of a non-Christian position with tremendous force to all who feel keenly the misery of the world. More vividly than anything else in the Old Testament, it shows us how imperious was the necessity for the revelation of God in Christ. There is much in the Old Testament from which a Christian instinctively recoils. It constitutes the dark background against which God has set the radiant figure of His Son, and it drives home to us with quite peculiar power how much the world needed the authentic voice to redress the balance and assure us that all is well.

CHAPTER EIGHT

Solution or Escape ?

THE problem of pain is of all problems the most baffling to many who wish to accept a theistic view of the universe. Even sin and death are mysteries less oppressive and impenetrable. If sin is a darker evil, pain is the more obscure. The freedom to choose the better, which confers all its moral worth on obedience to the Divine will, involves the freedom to choose the worse. It is, moreover, the natural impulse of every creature to seek its own ends, and seek them along its own lines. With inexperience and the inability to take long views, ith the overwhelming pressure of the physical and ternal, with all the inherited passion derived from untold ages of brute ancestry, we need not marvel that man seeks the immediate pleasure, and that his will should clash with the holy will of God. But does not this merely thrust the difficulty a stage farther back, and prove God at fault for so constituting man that sin was inevitable ? No doubt God must accept responsibility for His act, but how else was He to proceed ? The struggle must be real, if man's victory was to be of worth ; the dice must not be loaded in his favour. Was it not also more fit that man should have come to be by the slow escape from the brute's wholly finite and non-moral life into consciousness of a moral order and sense of the Divine, than that the continuity of life should be ruptured, and those elements in his nature which

have made his trial so severe have found no place in
a creature fresh from the hand of God ? For thus the
conditions in which he is to receive his moral discipline
are natural and not artificial.

And still less can death be called an evil. This is
obviously true as it affects the race. No death
would soon mean no birth ; those in possession
would prevent new comers from trenching on their
domain. Thus life with its blessings would be confined
to the few, instead of being distributed to many
swiftly succeeding generations. In such a world
progress would be inconceivably difficult, the dead
weight of custom would crush all aspirations to reform.
Even if fresh lives came into it, what could they do,
pitted against the tyranny of tradition backed by
power and the timidity of experience ? Far better
that death should remove the men callous to abuse
and hostile to reform, and that men of warmer
impulses, higher ideals, more generous enthusiasm
should fill their place. The treasures of the past
are not therefore lost, but made the solid basis for
future progress. And, even for the individual,
death is in itself no unhappy fate. It may be
untimely, it may be tragic, because it cuts short a
career full of promise, or robs the world of the fruits
of genius, or the harvest of long labour and research.
Or in other ways it may be invested through its
circumstances with evil in this form or that. But in
itself death should be a welcome guest. Immortality
of any kind would be no boon were not infinite
resources available to satisfy each new craving as
it arose. But physical immortality might well be
intolerable, the captive spirit for ever beating its
bars in vain, or the body weary of its burden and

unable to lay it down. Even if death meant complete extinction of being, there is in that nothing terrible. Nature, no doubt, secures the preservation of the species by the instinctive clinging to life which she has implanted in the individual. But the recoil from extinction, which springs from this instinct, gains all its force through an illusion, an unconscious contradiction. The pathos with which it is invested is due simply to this, that the individual unconsciously thinks himself back into existence to contemplate his own non-existence, he projects the feeling of revulsion that he experiences before the event, into the future when all power of contemplation and feeling has passed away. But in spite of our imagination the extinct person has no consciousness, and is not aware as the sentimentalist tricks himself into fancying, of the misery of his condition. How many tired workers, worn out with the unceasing strain on strength and brain and nerve, would sink gladly into a rest that should never again be disturbed by the call to labour or to pastime ! How many, whose days and nights stretch them on the rack of anguish, would hail the sleep that knows no waking, whether to pleasure or pain ! They are past caring for happiness, all that they crave is rest. It is the bereaved for whom death is a tragedy, but this aspect demands consideration rather as a form of suffering.

It is true that the mystery of suffering has its palliatives. Pain teaches us a tenderness and sympathy for those who suffer. It gives new care and watchfulness to our love, stimulates us to self-forgetfulness and helpful service. And if the contemplation of pain be thus beneficent, so too may be its endurance. Leaving aside the part it plays as a danger signal, pointing to mischief in the physical organism, that might do irreparable damage, if its insidious movement were not thus rudely detected, we know full well what noble spiritual ends it often serves. It disciplines our waywardness, convinces us by stern retribution how stringent a demand the order under which we live makes upon us, it sweetens the temper, softens and refines the character and braces the will. Even the shock of bereavement has in it some element of good. The knowledge that it may come checks the hasty and irretrievable word that may so soon torture us with vain regrets, it bids us love and serve our friends, ere they pass beyond our reach. And when they have left us, with what new sacredness and solemnity we cherish their memory. Death has disclosed to us their ideal significance, it has disengaged the essential spirit from earth's poor expression, the trivial and transient have fallen from them. The separations life has made, death has often healed.

But when all these things have been freely admitted, it is plain that they are quite inadequate to meet the appalling difficulties of the problem. Even to the palliatives mentioned there is another side. In some the contemplation of pain rouses irritation and disgust, while the endurance of it only exasperates and embitters them. The thought of possible bereavement darkens our lives with foreboding ; the experience, even if remorse be absent, bruises us where we are most sensitive, and often means the permanent impoverishment of our life. And when we turn our gaze to the world's actual misery, little as we know of it, we are overwhelmed by it, so innumerable, intolerable, inexcusable seem the pains of the sentient universe. The wrongs of the lower creation at the hands of Nature or of man, even though they are not intensified by suspense or magnified by anticipation and the faculty of connected thought, constitute in themselves a grave indictment against the morality of the order under which we live, all the more that, so far as we see, they serve few of the useful ends fulfilled by human pain. And who can number the wrongs of man ? Even in our softer and more humane age and country we are confronted by evils which strike horror into our hearts. And when we widen our outlook to take in those other lands, less happy even than our own, or peer into the past and scan the ages when brutal ferocity or malignant and ingenious cruelty reigned unchecked, we shudder and are dumb before the insolent cynicism which tramples so ruthlessly on its victims. The fiendish horrors in Armenia or Macedonia, or on the Congo ; the callous infliction of extreme pain by the highly civilized on the negro defrauded of human rights ; the nameless atrocities decreed by Persia to the followers of the Bab, all remind us with what slowness progress drags the reluctant nations in its train. Yet ghastly as are these deeds that stain humanity with indelible shame, they are but a small fraction of the woes, which through long ages have gnawed at the vitals of our hapless race. Think of the victims of superstition and blind terror in savage lands, of the tortures that, in the ages of judicial darkness and malignant bigotry, were made to serve the cause of justice or religion, think how the barbarities of an Assyrian emperor in honour of Asshur, were more than matched by the Inquisitor's nicely adjusted and elaborate

on an object other than Himself, but always in that ineffable and unthinkable life, where His Unity as God is not impaired by its inclusion of subject and object, there is the blessed communion of Father, Son, and Spirit. And this love, since it is love, seeks to create new objects, for it does not selfishly desire to restrict its boons, but rather to bring within the reach of its activities all that it may. This love is proved to us by a stupendous sacrifice, in that God gave us the eternal Son. With this assurance we can be at rest. For like Job we feel that our knowledge of God is that which we have heard ' by the hearing of the ear '. Nature and History alike speak to us with an ambiguous voice. With this hearsay knowledge of God we can reach no confident foothold. But to know Jesus is to know God ; when we see Him we can say to God : ' Now mine eye seeth Thee.' The Vision of God in Jesus brings us peace. All is well, we cannot say how, but we are certain of the fact.

But all this is true, only if Christianity is true, and if Jesus of Nazareth is the Son of God. It is not given to me to stand where many stand, to surrender a belief in His Divinity, and yet to hold fast a faith in God's goodness. The longer I ponder the world's pain in itself, the more it seems to deny a moral government of the world, and the more I feel drawn to the conviction that on this, the greatest of all questions, Ecclesiastes has said the last word. And if I do not yield to this temptation, it is because I ponder it also in the light of the Cross, on which the Son of God manifested the eternal love. When thus it is granted us to believe in Jesus, we take

courage to believe in God. But Jesus helps us in
our need, not only as the manifestation of God's love
but by His own unshaken faith. He knew the
sharp anguish of our lot, faced in all its gloom and
terror our deepest sorrow, made Himself one with us
in our bitterest suffering, endured, without flinching,
desertion, betrayal, torture, and death. Even in
that darker agony, so awful, so solitary, so mysterious,
that we turn dizzy as we gaze into its depths, He
called God His Father, and said : ' Thy will be
done ! '   If He who knew God, as no other has
known Him, could still in His desperate extremity
maintain His firm trust in God's goodness, how
much this strengthens our own wavering faith. Yet
how can we believe with Jesus unless we have come
to believe in Him ? If His Cross is not the key to
the riddle of the universe, it darkens the mystery,
and makes the travail of creation more unmeaning
than ever. But in the face of all our difficulties it
is no easy thing to believe in Jesus. We can realize
better now than in some ages how true are the words:
' No man can say Jesus is Lord but in the Holy
Spirit.' But when once by the grace of God we
have dared to make this great affirmation, then
we enter into His unspeakable peace. The world's
sorrows do not cease to be terrible, and to wring
our hearts, we feel them with all the deeper sympathy
and inspired by Christ's Spirit, long to relieve
them. We understand them but little better, nor
can we reconcile them successfully with the love
of God. Mystery still besets us behind and before,
and all we comprehend of God's work in the universe
is ' but the outskirts of His ways '. Yet we know
in whom we have believed, and if we know that,

all our ignorance is insignificant. That knowledge takes us to the centre, and we feel the love that throbs at the heart of creation. We leave our unravelled perplexities behind us; they have fallen from us, and can dismay us no longer. We do not ask the answer, we are content not to know. For no unriddling of the mystery can bring us a peace more unruffled than that in which we rest on the bosom of God, that strong Magician, who, with the wand of His love, has charmed into quiet the doubts that once surged so tempestuously in our breast.

Recent Criticism of Habakkuk

WE MAY conveniently take the brief discussion in Giesebrecht's *Beiträge zur Jesaiakritik*, published in 1891, as our point of departure for the criticism of Habakkuk 1^1-2^8. This section had previously been regarded as in its right order, and it had been commonly thought that in 1^{2-4} the prophet complains of the violence of Jewish oppressors in Judah, in 1^{5-11} receives the revelation that Yahweh is about to raise up the Chaldeans to punish them, while in the rest of the section, Habakkuk complains of the tyranny of the Chaldeans and receives the assurance that the righteous shall live by his faithfulness, but the tyrant shall be overthrown by the nations he has spoiled. This view, however, was open to the serious, and probably fatal, objection, that it identified ' the wicked ' in 1^{2-4} with Jewish sinners, whereas in 1^{12-17} ' the wicked ' can only be the heathen oppressor. Accordingly some scholars (e.g. Wellhausen in 1873) had abandoned this double interpretation, and argued that both in 1^{2-4} and in 1^{12-17} the prophet is complaining that righteous Judah is suffering at the hands of the heathen tyrant. This tyrant was on all hands supposed to be the Chaldean power. But if we identify 'the wicked ' in 1^{2-4} with those in 1^{12-17}, and regard the Chaldeans as intended in both, then 1^2-2^3 cannot be explained as it stands. For while $1^{2-4,\ 12-17}$ represents the oppression as long-established, 1^{5-11}

represents the Chaldeans as just being raised up to do an incredible work. It was the merit of Giesebrecht to draw the inference that 1^{5-11} could not be in its true context, since it presupposed a situation altogether incompatible with that reflected in $1^{2-4, \; 12-17}$. He assigned the section $1^{1}-2^{8}$ with the exception of 1^{5-11} to the Exile, and 1^{5-11} he assigned to an earlier period, when the Chaldeans were beginning their career of conquest. In 1892 Wellhausen accepted Giesebrecht's conclusion that 1^{5-11} was no part of the original prophecy, as the necessary inference from his own earlier position (*Die Kleinen Propheten*, note on Habakkuk 1^{5-11}). But he thought that the section ended with 2^{4}, and as we may infer from his note on 2^{15-17}, regarded $1^{2-4, \; 12-17}$ and 2^{1-4} as pre-exilic. The prophecy, as thus limited, seemed too meagre in its teaching to have needed a revelation.

Meanwhile Budde had independently worked out a wholly new theory, which he published in *Studien und Kritiken* (1893), pp. 383 ff. He also had observed that 1^{5-11} is out of place where it stands, but did not on that account eliminate it as a foreign element. Its proper place he argued was at the end of the section, after 2^{4}. For in this way we have the prediction of judgement following the description of tyranny, a natural order. But, if so, then the Chaldeans cannot be the oppressor, rather they are raised up to take vengeance upon him. It followed therefore that two heathen nations were referred to, one in 1^{2-4}, $1^{12}-2^{4}$, the oppressor, and the other in 1^{5-11} (or as Budde held 1^{6-11}), the Chaldean avenger. Budde thus reached the completely new theory that the oppressor was Judah's old tyrant

Assyria, and that Habakkuk about 615 B.C. predicted the overthrow of Assyria by the nascent power of the Chaldeans. He has further expounded his theory in the *Expositor* (May 1895), and most recently in his article ' Habakkuk ' in the *Encyclopædia Biblica*. Cornill adopted it in the next edition of his ' Introduction to the Old Testament ' (*Einleitung in das A.T.*[3-4] (1896), pp. 194-5), and his popular lectures on Hebrew Prophecy (*Das israelitsche Prophetismus* (1894) pp. 79-80: E.T., *The Prophets of Israel*). It has, however, been rejected by A. B. Davidson ('Nahum, Habakkuk, and Zephaniah' in *The Cambridge Bible* (1895), pp. 50-5, 139), by Driver (*Introduction to the Literature of the Old Testament*, Sixth Edition (1897), p. 338, ' too ingenious '), and by Nowack (*Die Kleinen Propheten* (1897), pp. 248-50, 259, 260).

In the third edition of his commentary on the Minor Prophets (1898), Wellhausen abides by the view taken in the first, and ignores Budde's theory. On the other hand three scholars have accepted his view that the Chaldeans are raised up to execute judgement on a heathen oppressor. G. A. Smith (*Book of the Twelve Prophets*, Vol. II (1898), pp. 123-4), feeling the difficulties urged against the view that this oppressor was Assyria, suggested that the prophet may have intended Egypt, which for a few years ruled over Judah. Quite recently Peiser, the well-known Assyriologist, has made an entirely new suggestion (' Der Prophet Habakuk' in *Mitteilungen der Vorderasiatischen Gesellschaft* for 1903, No. 1). Habakkuk criticism has, he thinks, reached a deadlock, and, if progress toward a true solution is to be made, new methods must be employed.

He has been struck with parallels between the prophecy and Assyrian and Babylonian literature, of a kind to suggest that the prophet had some familiarity with this literature and had studied it in the cuneiform script. This would have been possible to a resident in Jerusalem, but there is no reference to Judah, and naturally it is more easily explicable in a writer who lived in Assyria or Babylonia. And that the author was in a foreign land he infers from the amended text of 3¹⁶. He assigns to Habakkuk, against the usual critical view, the third chapter, but agress with Wellhausen that the original poem does not go beyond verse 16. In that case, he argues the prophecy cannot have ended with an indeterminate 'am (' people '), followed by an indeterminate relative sentence. Accordingly for the final word in our present text, *yegudennū*, which is a well-known *crux*, he substitutes, following the LXX and the Syriac Codex Ambrosianus, *mᵉgūray*, gaining the sense, ' which cometh up against the people of my sojourning '. If this was the original text, the writer would at the time be in a foreign land. In 3¹³ the poet says : ' Thou wentest forth for the salvation of Thy people, For the salvation of Thine anointed.' Peiser thinks that by ' Thine anointed ' the poet meant himself. He infers that he was a hostage at Nineveh, a Jewish prince who, as Yahweh's anointed, had a right to the Jewish throne. Perhaps he was a son or grandson of Manasseh. He would be brought up in the fashion usual at the court of Nineveh, and was probably keenly interested in the library formed by Assurbanipal. The prophecy is left by Peiser in its present order. He agrees with Budde that the Chaldeans are named as the instruments of Yahweh's judgement on the Assyrians. But he regards the violence, of which the prophet complains, as violence in Nineveh, not in Judah, and he takes 1^{5-11} to refer to a past attack of the Chaldeans on Assyria, which from 1^{11} he infers to have been abortive. The prophet looks forward to a second attack on Assyria, which he expects to be successful. The former attack is identified with the first onslaught of the Medes against Nineveh, repulsed in 625 B.C. with the death of the Median prince. The date of the prophecy is fixed about 609. Probably the news of Josiah's death excited this outcry against the power which kept the author from his rights.

A modification of Budde's theory has been proposed by Prof. W. R. Betteridge, of Rochester Theological Seminary, in the *American Journal of Theology* for October 1903. He thinks that the Chaldeans are raised up to execute Yahweh's vengeance on the Assyrians. But he argues that Budde's date is impossible, and that we must go back to a period when the hand of Assyria pressed heavily on Judah. Since, however, Judah is represented as at the time a righteous nation, we cannot assign the prophecy to the reign of Manasseh or the early years of Josiah, but must go back to the time of Hezekiah and date it after his reform. He fixes on 701 B.C. when Sennacherib was recalled from his invasion of Judah by tidings of a revolt in Babylonia. He attributes the whole book to Habakkuk, and retains the present order.

In estimating these theories, the point that seems to be best established is that 'the wicked' in 1^{2-4} must be identified with 'the wicked' in 1^{12-17}. In other words, Habakkuk does not complain that wicked

Jews oppress their righteous countrymen, but that a heathen nation oppresses righteous Judah. Although Davidson and Driver do not admit this, they feel that the usual view is not altogether satisfactory, but adopt it because it seems the best way to take the passage as it stands, and Budde's rearrangement is for various reasons unsatisfactory. If, then, I venture to dissent from their conclusion it is in deference to arguments which they admit to be cogent. If, further, mention is made of one heathen power only in 1^{2-17}, that power must be the Chaldean. But the inference of Giesebrecht and Wellhausen is then inevitable, that 1^{5-11} is an earlier prophecy which is out of place in this context. Such a solution cuts the knot, instead of untying it, but if none of the other solutions commend themselves, it is on it that we are driven back. If the Chaldeans are the subject of $1^{2-4, \; 12-17}$, then these passages reflect a situation incompatible with that reflected in 1^{5-11}. Naturally, however, this is a last resort, to be accepted only if the ascription of 1^{5-11} to Habakkuk should prove to be untenable.

It is the merit of Budde's theory and the modifications of it, that it permits us to regard 1^{5-11} as an integral part of the prophecy ; but it cannot be denied that each form of the theory is open to serious objections. Those of Budde and G. A. Smith labour under the initial difficulty that they postulate a dislocation of the original prophecy. This is not at all a fatal objection. It is very probable that originally Isaiah 5^{25-30} stood in connexion with Isaiah 9^8-10^4. Moreover Budde explains that in the present case the dislocation was intentional. After the Chaldeans became the oppressing power and had been overthrown, the prediction of their rise was transferred from its original position after 2^4 to its present position between 1^4 and 1^{12}, and thus in the fifth or fourth century the prophecy was turned into an oracle against Babylon. I must confess that this explanation would seem to me more credible, if I could credit the ancient editor with the ingenious subtlety of the distinguished modern critic. I should prefer to assume that as in Isaiah 5^{25-30} accident rather than design had been at work. In the next place all theories that regard the Chaldeans as raised up to punish another heathen nation, labour under the difficulty that while the Chaldeans are named, the empire they are to destroy is not. Budde, it is true, supposes that Asshur stood originally in 1^{11} (instead of $w^e\bar{a}shem$) : ' Then shall disappear like the wind, and pass away, Asshur who has made his strength his god.' The text of 1^{11} is notoriously difficult, but although Budde's suggestion deserves consideration, the objection remains that in our present text, the oppressing empire is not named. This, however, is not a very serious difficulty. On the view of Peiser or Betteridge, the reference to Assyria would be so clear that no need to mention it by name would be felt. And even on Budde's theory there was no such necessity ; who the oppressor was, would be understood by the people as well as by the prophet. Similar phenomena are not uncommon. Amos does not name Assyria as the power which is to inflict judgement on Israel, nor does Isaiah in the great passage 5^{26-30}. It is still a matter of dispute whether it was the Assyrian army or the combined forces of Syria and Ephraim whose ravages are depicted in Isaiah 1. It is quite uncertain

reasonable to complain because matters were not righted all at once. Probably Judah was not in a miserable condition at all, but rather, with the relaxing grip of Assyria and Josiah's virtual independence, the years in question were among the happiest in the nation's history.

On the other hand, Budde's view has some advantages. Wellhausen's feeling that the result reached in 2^4 is too meagre to be worthy of a revelation has considerable force ; we should have expected a prediction of judgement on the oppressor. This is met if we allow 1^{6-11} to follow. There is also something to be said for Budde's contention that the methods of conquest described in 1^{12-17} are those adopted by Assyria rather than by the Chaldeans : ' Not all at once, but by numerous separate efforts spread over three centuries, not merely by force of arms, but (as the angling metaphor suggests) by policy and craft, were so many petty principalities and more than one important kingdom swept into the hands of these robbers (cf. Isaiah $10^{5-11, \, 13f}$). The Chaldean, on the other hand, far from being the unresting persistent, grasping, amasser of wealth, was simply the smiling heir ' (Encyclopædia Biblica, column 1923).

Prof. G. A. Smith escapes the worst difficulty of Budde's view, inasmuch as the circumstances, out of which he thinks the prophecy springs, were such as to create its problem. The death of Josiah on the battlefield, the loss of virtual independence, the captivity of Jehoahaz, were all so many inexplicable mysteries on the deeply-rooted belief that character and fortune closely corresponded. The date would then have to lie between 609 and 605 B.C

It is in the earlier rather than in the later part of this period that we should probably have to fix it, before Jehoiakim had had time to display his evil qualities, and before the Reformation had been undone, while men were still stunned by the tragedy of Josiah's death and the disasters that so quickly followed it. But the objections to this view are weighty. Dr. Smith himself suggests one : ' But then does the description in chapter 1[14–17] suit Egypt so well as it does Assyria ? We can hardly affirm this, until we know more of what Egypt did in those days, but it is very probable ' (page 124). This is very dubious, but, even if it be granted, there is a further difficulty. The prophecy leaves a very strong impression that the evil of which the prophet complains is one of long standing. He begins with the question : ' How long, O Yahweh, shall I cry and Thou wilt not hear ? ' In 1[17] he not only asks, ' And shall He not spare to slay the nations continually ', but also, if with Wellhausen, Nowack, and G. A. Smith himself, we accept an emendation of Giesebrecht (*Beiträge*, page 197, n. 1), and read *ha'ōlam* for *ha'al kēn*, ' shall he for ever be emptying his net ? ' This surely points to a condition of things that had been going on for a much longer period than the four years, which is all that this view permits.

Peiser's theory shares with Budde's the advantage that it identifies the oppressor with the long-triumphant power of Assyria, and escapes Budde's most formidable difficulty by transferring the centre of interest from Palestine to Nineveh. The lion was formidable in his own lair (Nahum 2[11–13]), after his distant dominion had vanished. There can also on this theory be no difficulty raised by 1²⁻⁴, the violence of which the prophet complains is not in Judah, but the tyranny practised in Nineveh by the Assyrians. How far the arguments based on the author's familiarity with Assyrian and Babylonian literature are valid, is for cuneiform scholars to say, and this applies also to the suggestion (page 12), that Habakkuk might well be an Assyrian pseudonym. Friedrich Delitzsch had previously given the same derivation. Naturally much depends on this for a decision on the theory that the prophet wrote in Nineveh, and till specialists have pronounced their opinion, judgement must remain to some extent in suspense. The author, however, does not himself affirm that familiarity with the literature of Assyria and Babylon in cuneiform script necessarily implies residence in one of these countries. It would be consistent with residence in Jerusalem (page 10). Nevertheless, if it could be made out, the opinion that he lived in Nineveh would gain in probability. The other argument by which this is substantiated is precarious. It rests on the assumption that the third chapter is by Habakkuk, and this is denied by a large number of scholars. A second assumption is that the original poem ended at verse 16. It was suggested by Wellhausen that the original conclusion was lost and 3¹⁷⁻¹⁹ substituted for it. He is followed by Nowack (page 248), while Davidson, though thinking this quite possible, pronounces no definite opinion. It is, however, unfavourably regarded by Budde and rejected by G. A. Smith. Peiser's interpretation of 3¹⁶ has, of course, independent support in the difficulty of the present text, and the translation given by the LXX   It would be strengthened, however, if 3^{17-19} were a later addition. Peiser differs from Wellhausen in holding that the poem originally closed with verse 16, and that the original ending has not been lost, verses 17–19 being simply an addition, not a substitution. If this could be proved, it would be difficult to defend our present text. Even so, it is unsafe to build a theory on an emendation, though supported by the LXX. The reference of ' Thine anointed ' in 3^{13} to the prophet himself as the rightful monarch is very dubious. The parallelism favours the usual interpretation of the term as the people of Yahweh, a usage which belongs to the period after the destruction of the monarchy. Peiser's view of 1^{5-11} is also very questionable. The passage does not make the impression that it refers to an event now sixteen years old. Rather it is some impending catastrophe that is to be brought about by the rise of the Chaldeans And if 1^5 is to be closely connected with what follows, this work which Yahweh is to perform through the Chaldeans is declared to be of an incredible character It is not at all clear how Peiser interprets 1^5, except that he does not regard it as part of the speech of Yahweh, announcing that the Chaldeans are to be raised up. But it is plain why he has reached the conclusion that 1^{6-11} refers to an event in 625, though he does not explain it. He believes that Habakkuk wrote about 609 B.C. But it would be absurd for anyone writing in Nineveh at that time to speak of the Chaldeans as just being raised up. Since Nabopolassar, the Chaldean monarch, had united Babylonians and Chaldeans in 625, and had made good his claims to the throne of Babylon, the Chaldeans had been a standing menace to the

Assyrian empire. That the attack on Nineveh in 625 was a failure is inferred from 1[11], a passage the meaning of which is so uncertain, that nothing can safely be proved by it. What is strange, however, is that the prophet, if he had this attack in mind, and had himself lived through it, should speak of it as if it had been made by the Chaldeans. They may have been in alliance with the Medes, but it was the Medes who actually struck at Nineveh. If we are to think of the prophecy as having been written in Nineveh, it would seem to be much sounder to carry the matter through to a more logical conclusion and date it shortly before 625.

The view taken by Prof. Betteridge is at first sight very attractive. It is not, as with Budde's theory, with the numb grip of a decadent Assyria, but with Assyria in full career of conquest that the prophet is confronted. As he looks from the still uncaptured Jerusalem on a land laid waste and trampled by a brutal soldiery, its towns and fortresses all taken, with innumerable captives and an enormous spoil, the thought may well have risen within him, Why does Yahwch abandon His people to the heathen ? Hitherto it has been generally assumed that the prophecy must be later than 621 B.C., because only after Josiah's reformation could Judah have been described as a righteous people. But why not equally well after Hezekiah's reformation ? It is no objection to this that the latter did not take place at the instigation of a law. Even if the prophecy is post-Deuteronomic there is no need to suppose that *torah* in 1[4] refers to the Deuteronomic Code. The omission of the article and the parallelism with *misphāt* (judgement) suggests rather that it is to

be taken in a more general sense, and we may translate ' truth ' with Wellhausen and Nowack, or explain
it with Betteridge to refer to moral and social order.
If the prophecy belongs to Hezekiah's reign, then
obviously *torah* no more means ' law ' here than
it does in the contemporary passage, Isaiah 1[10].
Moreover, the words ' Behold I raise up the Chaldeans '
get a fuller significance on this view than on any
other. The Chaldeans who are not to be identified
with the Babylonians, really became formidable
toward the close of the eighth century B.C. It
was not so correct to speak of them a century later
as being raised up. For a time the Chaldean
Merodach-Baladan achieved remarkable success. He
was well known in Judah, to which he had sent
ambassadors, no doubt with a view to combined
action against Assyria. At that time expectation
may well have been formed that the Chaldeans
were designed to overthrow Assyria. In spite,
however, of these real advantages, it is very difficult
to accept this view at any rate in its present
form.

In the first place Habakkuk is generally regarded
as strongly influenced by Isaiah. But we know
what Isaiah thought of Judah and its treatment
at Assyria's hands in 701. We find it in 22[1-14] and
probably in 1[2-28]. True, he held firm to his belief in
the indestructibility of Zion, which was a corollary
to his belief that Yahweh dwelt in it. And he expected
Assyria to be destroyed, not for its treatment of
Judah, but for its arrogance and its blasphemy
against Yahweh. This has its parallel in Habakkuk
2[4] and perhaps 1[11]. But the suffering of Judah is
no problem to Isaiah ; she has richly deserved it all.

And he does not look for Assyria to be overthrown by human power. He steadily discourages all foreign alliances for that purpose, and anticipates that Assyria will be broken on the mountains of Yahweh. It may, no doubt, be urged that the difficulty created by the peculiar stand-point of Habakkuk is just as great on any theory, since Jeremiah as much as Isaiah regards the sorrows of Judah as the due reward of her deeds. It would, however, be very remarkable if in 701 Isaiah and a prophet so influenced by him as Habakkuk spoke in such different tones. Might it not be preferable to place it nearer the reformation, when the glow of conscious virtue had not been chilled by its disappointing sequel? Moreover, it is very difficult on historical grounds to believe that the prophecy could have originated in 701. For it was only in the previous year that Sennacherib had driven Merodach-Baladan out of Babylon, and had punished Chaldea with great severity. ' Cities to the number of seventy-five in Chaldea proper, with four hundred and twenty neighbouring villages were taken and spoiled ' (M'Curdy, *History, Prophecy, and the Monuments*, Volume II, page 274). Is it likely that just then any prophet in Judah should have anticipated that the Chaldeans would overthrow Assyria? It is true that Sennacherib seems to have been recalled from his campaign in Judah by news of a revolt in Babylonia. We may accept this on the basis of Isaiah 37[7], without committing ourselves to the theory, now favoured by several scholars, that there was a second invasion by Sennacherib some time between 690 and 681 ' Hope springs eternal ', and Judah may have looked once more to the Chaldeans for deliverance. If so, she was bitterly disappointed, for Sennacherib attacked Bit Yakin in 700, when Merodach-Baladan fled with all the gods of his land to Nagitu in the Fens, an Elamite city, which was captured by Sennacherib, in 694 B.C. It would probably be an improvement on this theory to place the prophecy earlier in Hezekiah's reign, when negotiations with the Chaldeans gave promise of the oppressor's downfall. All through the period from 735, when Ahaz took the fateful step of invoking the aid of Tiglath Pileser to suppress the coalition of Syria and Ephraim, the hand of Assyria pressed heavily on the unhappy land. And, to say nothing of earlier Chaldean success, from the time of Sargon's accession in 721 till 710 Merodach-Baladan held the throne of Babylon. During those years he may well have seemed the destined conqueror of Assyria. Or we might think of the second occasion when he seized Babylon in 703 or 702, when Hezekiah also was throwing off the Assyrian yoke. There is, however, no suggestion in the prophecy that Judah is planning to strike a blow for freedom, and 1^{6-11} does not make the impression that the Chaldeans had only recently received a severe check. It might be urged against a date in Hezekiah's reign that there are several parallels with Jeremiah. But this is one of those arguments of which we do well to be distrustful. It is generally thought that the description of the Chaldeans in 1^{6-11} exhibits traits borrowed from the Scythians. If it is as late as the reign of Josiah this is probable. Winckler, indeed, supposes that it was an oracle referring to the Scythians. But he takes the same view also of Isaiah 5^{25-30}. The description might suit the Chaldeans better in the

eighth century than in the time of Nabopolassar
and Nebuchadnezzar.

Grave difficulties lie therefore against every form of
the view that the Chaldeans are raised up to inflict
Yahweh's judgement on another heathen power,
though it would be an advantage if we could seek
for a solution along this line, inasmuch as the prophecy
gains a completeness which it does not posesss if
we simply eliminate 1⁵⁻¹¹. Nor can we shut our
eyes to the difficulties that may be urged against
the latter view. If the prophet is complaining in
1²⁻⁴,¹²⁻¹⁷, of Chaldean tyranny, we are obliged to
bring the prophecy well below 605 B.C., for the
prophet speaks out of no little experience of it. But
during the whole period from 605 to the fall of
Jerusalem in 586, it would be far less fitting to speak
of Judah as righteous than in the days of Josiah.
Might we then with Giesebrecht place its origin in
the Exile? This seems at first sight to be unlikely
since there is no allusion to the captivity, or to the
destruction of city and temple. It is not an insuperable objection. We have a parallel in Isaiah 13,
though the author of this passage has very little to
say of the wrongs inflicted by Babylon, his attention
being almost wholly engrossed by the doom in store
for it. The possibility of an exilic date has been
very little discussed. Budde says the prophecy
must be pre-exilic, but his reason is simply that 1²⁻⁴
presupposes the existence of the kingdom of Judah.
It is not easy to see why. It might just as well
refer to the oppressive treatment of the Jews in
exile. Baudissin makes a similar objection. There
is moreover a positive advantage in an exilic date.
The character of prophecy largely changed with

the destruction of Jerusalem. Before it the prophets
for the most part spoke of judgement on the people
of Yahweh, after it they were in the main messengers
of consolation to Judah and of judgement on the
heathen. Habakkuk belongs to the latter type.
This does not prove that he prophesied after the
destruction of Jerusalem. But we have already
seen that every pre-exilic date proposed is open to
serious objections. And we know that after the blow
had fallen, Judah developed a consciousness of her
own righteousness, at least a relative righteousness
over against the heathen. If we thought of the
prophecy as written in exile, this might account
for the parallels with cuneiform literature pointed
out by Peiser. We might then with Lauterburg
(*Theol. Z. aus d. Schweiz* (1896), pp. 24 ff.) read
'Persians' for 'Chaldeans' in 1^6 and retain 1^{5-11}
as a prediction that judgement will be executed on
the Chaldeans by the Persians. But this is very
improbable, for it is not easy to see why anyone
should have changed 'Persians' into 'Chaldeans',
since such a change would have been in the wrong
direction. It is more probable, however, that 1^{5-11}
should be regarded as an independent prophecy
dating from the pre-exilic period, when the Chaldeans
were striking into the larger currents of history. For
it is difficult to regard it as belonging to the original
prophecy, inasmuch as in 2^3 there are obviously no
circumstances in sight to suggest the speedy
disappearance of the oppressor, which is, as Wellhausen says, 'only a moral postulate'. It reminds
us of 'I the Lord will hasten it in its time' (Isaiah
60^{22}).

If then though with misgivings, we regard 1^{2-4}

and $1^{12}-2^4$, as originating in the Exile, a suggestion
may be made with a view to determine more narrowly
the limits of date.   The lower limit is given us by
the fact, to which allusion has just been made,
that no definite circumstances are on the prophet's
horizon, pointing to the overthrow of the Babylonian
empire.   Accordingly we cannot place it much, if
any, later than 546.   On the other hand the absence
of allusion to the captivity and the sack of Jerusalem
is most easily accounted for if we suppose that the
prophet had not lived through them, or was too
young at the time to remember them.   If he went
as a child to Babylonia with Jehoiachin in 597 or
was born in Babylonia soon after, as is more likely,
he could very well have seen his vision thirty or forty
years later.   If we date the prophecy about 560–550,
we shall not perhaps be far from the mark.   We
cannot well place it in the post-exilic period,
for the problem is in a rudimentary stage, and the
author has hardly behind him the discussion of it
in Isaiah 40–55.

It will not be necessary to add much on the
remaining sections of the prophecy.   Against the
view of Stade and Kuenen that the whole of 2^{9-20}
is a post-exilic addition the reader may consult the
discussions of Davidson, G. A. Smith, and Driver
(Hastings' *Dictionary of the Bible*), or the detailed
defence in Smend's *Alttestamentliche Religionsgeschichte* (First Edition (1893), pp. 229–30 : It is not
repeated in the second edition.)   Most of the scholars
who have written on the subject recently think
that part at any rate of the section comes from
Habakkuk.

Wellhausen thinks the whole of the woes were uttered

against the Chaldeans, but 12–14 have been put together from Micah 3[10], Jeremiah 51[58] and Isaiah 11[9], while 15–17 cannot well come from a prophet who prophesied before the exile since it rests on Jeremiah 25. On 2[18–20] he simply says that 19 should precede 18, and that 20 clearly prepares the way for the Theophany in chapter 3. This would involve our treating 20 as a later addition, but no opinion is expressed on the authorship of verses 19 and 18. I suspect from the reference to Isaiah 41 that Wellhausen regards them as late exilic. Nowack regards 12–14, 18 and 20 as later additions, 9–11, 15, 16 and 17a as by Habakkuk ; 19 is viewed with suspense, though printed as an addition in the translation. Budde thinks 12–14 and 18–20 are later additions. Cornill further suspects 15–17 in its present form. G. A. Smith rejects 18–20, and is doubtful about 12–14. If, however, we date Habakkuk's prophecy in the exile, there is no reason why all the woes in the second chapter should not have come from him, though 12–14 is possibly later. On 20, Budde's judgement may be quoted : ' It closes the passage not unfittingly but perhaps was intended at the same time to prepare for the Theophany in chapter 3.'

The third chapter is held by an increasing number of critics to be post-exilic, though its authorship by Habakkuk is defended by Kirkpatrick and Betteridge, and, with the exception of 17–19, by Peiser. It is not necessary for the present purpose to discuss the question. Stade, Kuenen, and Wellhausen have done most to substantiate the view that it is a post-exilic Psalm. The arguments for this conclusion, which is probably correct, may be conveniently seen in Hastings' *Dictionary of the Bible* or the *Encyclopædia Biblica*.

[I have felt it unnecessary to state or discuss Rothstein's very ingenious theories of the first two chapters. I gave an outline of them in my *Guide to Biblical Study*, page 85. A full statement and criticism may be found in Budde's article in the *Expositor* for May 1895. So far as I know, they have met with no acceptance.]

Critical Problems of Isaiah 40—66

FOR the sake of those who are quite unfamiliar with the modern criticism of the Book of Isaiah, it is perhaps desirable to begin by justifying the view that the last twenty-seven chapters of the book cannot be assigned to Isaiah. Our present question is not whether these chapters themselves form a unity, but whether they can be ascribed to the main author of the earlier portion of the book. It is almost conclusive as an answer to this that the standpoint of the prophecy is not that of Isaiah's time but that of the Exile. And the prophet does not give any hint that this standpoint is assumed rather than real. There is no prediction of the Exile, it is described as having already for some time continued. The frequently repeated statement that an unbelief in the possibility of predictive prophecy underlies the denial of these chapters to Isaiah is therefore both untrue and irrelevant. For we have nothing to do with a prediction of the Exile and Return as still future, as they were to Isaiah, but a statement that the Jews are in exile and a prediction of their release. The evidence on this point may be first summarized. The prophecy opens with a message of comfort to the people of God and to Jerusalem, on the ground that the latter has received at the hands of Yahweh double punishment for all her sins. Jacob is saying despairingly that all his ways are hid from Yahweh, 40²⁷ Zion says Yahweh has forgotten me 49[14].   Jerusalem is drunk with the cup of His fury 51[17-23].   She is a captive with bands about her neck 52[2].   She has been forsaken and hated and her land is desolate 60[15], 62[4], 49[19].   The holy people have possessed their land but a little while, their adversaries have trodden down the sanctuary 63[18].   The holy cities are become a wilderness, Jerusalem a desolation.   The holy and beautiful house where their fathers praised Yahweh is burned with fire 64[10-11].   The oppressing power is Babylon, which has shown the people of God no mercy 47[6]. Israel is in exile in Babylon 48[20], it is a people robbed and spoiled, snared in holes and hid in prison houses, 42[22].   Such is the state of things described in the last twenty-seven chapters as actually existing.   But signs are already present that it is quickly coming to an end.   A mighty conqueror has been raised up from the East and the North, 41[2, 8, 25], 46[11], named Cyrus 44[28], 45[1].   The writer seems to point to his rise as the fulfilment of prophecies formerly given, 42[9], and in this fulfilment he bids his readers recognize the proof of Yahweh's power to predict the future. He does not predict the raising up of Cyrus as something that still lies in the future.   He has already begun his career of conquest, and attracted attention.   And if the view is right as it seems to be, that the former prophecies now fulfilled related to his rise, it is impossible to place the prophet's standpoint elsewhere than toward the close of the Exile, for he could not appeal to events still in the future as proofs that the prediction of them had been fulfilled.   While then the former prophecies have been fulfilled in that Cyrus has begun his career of conquest, this prophet has new things to declare, that Cyrus will overthrow Babylon and set the captives free, 43[14], 47, 48[14], 45[4, 13]. Following this comes the return of the exiles. They are bidden go forth from Babylon and flee from the Chaldeans 48[20]. The ransomed of Yahweh are to return and come with singing unto Zion 51[11]. Cyrus will say that Jerusalem shall be rebuilt and the foundation of the Temple be laid 44[28]. The cities of Judah shall also be built and the waste places restored 44[26], 61[3].

It is quite clear from this survey of the actual statements of these chapters that they cannot be earlier than toward the close of the Exile and that some at least are not later than the capture of Babylon by Cyrus in 538. But there are other important arguments proving that they cannot come from Isaiah. There are marked differences in theological ideas. Isaiah is mainly a prophet of judgement, while these chapters contain chiefly messages of comfort and prophecies of restoration. Isaiah's Messianic king disappears and the Servant of Yahweh, the missionary to the heathen and the martyr, a figure unknown to Isaiah, takes his place. The thought of Yahweh's greatness as displayed in creation is developed very fully but is absent from Isaiah. Isaiah's attitude to the Sabbath, 1[13], is not such as we find in 56[2-6], 58[13]. The idea of the remnant, while not completely absent, is very subordinate, whereas it holds a leading place in Isaiah's thought. The style of the later chapters is also very different from that of Isaiah, being more diffuse, rhetorical, and pathetic, nobly eloquent it is true, but circling rather monotonously around a few great thoughts. And the vocabulary, apart from the common stock of words in which two writers might easily coincide, presents very little that points to identity of authorship, and much that tells strongly the other way. These arguments which are much strengthened by detailed comparison of the two sections of the book may suffice to prove that these chapters are not from the hand of Isaiah.

The next question is whether Isaiah 40–66 forms, apart from slight interpolations, a substantial unity. It was natural that for a long period this assumption should pass unchallenged. Such scholars as Ewald and Bleek had, however, pointed out signs of composite authorship, and at a later period Cheyne opened the way to the newer criticism by his important article on Isaiah in the *Encyclopædia Britannica* (1881). Kuenen in his *Introduction to the Prophets* (1889) took up a very advanced position. The prophecy of Restoration he defined as consisting of chapters 40–9, 52^{1-12}, with possibly 52^{13}–53^{12}. In 1891 Cheyne reached the conclusion that the work of the Second Isaiah consisted of two parts : (a) 40–8, (b) a broken collection composed of 49^1 52^{12}, 52^{13}–53^{12} (a later addition by the author), 54, 55, 56^9–57^{21} (beginning with a long passage from an older prophet probably worked up with a Deutero-Isaianic fragment by the editor), and 60–2. In other words the Second Isaiah's work consisted of 40–55, 60–2, with part of 56^9–57^{21}. The question passed into a new stage with Duhm's commentary in 1892. He attributed 40–55, with the omission of the Servant passages, to the Second Isaiah, and 56–66 to a single author whom he called Trito-Isaiah. His results were very widely accepted with the exception of his view of the Servant passages. Cheyne, in his *Introduction to the Book of Isaiah* (1895), agreed that the work of the Second Isaiah did not extend beyond 55, but he thought that the Servant passages were inserted by the author and possibly were earlier compositions of his own. He further refused to admit the unity of 56–66. These chapters he regarded as containing ten independent compositions, not necessarily by so many authors, written in the age of Nehemiah, while 63^7–64^{12} he assigned to the time of Artaxerxes Ochus. Marti agrees with Duhm both as to the Second and Third Isaiah, except that he considers the Servant passages to be an integral part of the Second Isaiah's work. Since the publication of his *Introduction*, Cheyne has modified his view of 40–55 in two respects. In agreement with Kosters he considers that the Second Isaiah's work does not extend beyond 48, a position to which Kuenen approximated in his *Introduction*. 49–55 he regards as a post-exilic appendix. Further, he now considers the Servant passages to be post-exilic compositions.

The ground on which it is held that the last twenty-seven chapters are not a unity are very cogent, though it is not so clear where the line should be drawn between the work of the Second Isaiah and that of later supplementers. The case seems clearest against 65 and 66, least clear against 60–62. It is not possible to go through the various sections in detail, but since it is now commonly held that 56–66 are not by the Second Isaiah, it will be most convenient to begin by exhibiting the arguments that point to this conclusion. In the first place it would seem that there had been a restoration of exiles already (56^8). Some had already been gathered, and it is promised that others shall be gathered to these. This suits no period except after the return under Cyrus. The references to a return as still future in $60^{4, 8, 9}$, and 66^{20} do not conflict with this, for the return under Cyrus, and, much later, that under Ezra were comparatively small. The reference to all the nations in 66^{20} shows that the author is thinking of the Dispersion. This argument, however, does not prove that 56^{8} is not by the Second Isaiah. He might quite well have returned in 536 and added prophecies to those he had uttered in the Exile. Such a view would also be consistent with the fact that the Temple seems from some passages to have been rebuilt. The clearest instances are 65^{11} and 66^{6}, but it is also probable that 56^{5-7}, 60^{7}, 62^{9}, should be similarly interpreted. This brings us down to the year 515. The references to idolatry in 57^{3-14} and in the last two chapters, $65^{1-7, 11-12}$, and $66^{3-4, 17}$, scarcely suit the Exile. It was in fact one of the arguments, by which conservative critics defended the Isaianic authorship, that 57^{5-6} could not have been written in Babylon, where there are no torrent-beds or terebinths, but must have been written in Palestine. The rites described are also similar to those familiar in Canaanite worship. On this ground several critics supposed that 57^{3-14} was a pre-exilic passage inserted by the Second Isaiah. But it is far from clear why he should have inserted it, and the tone of the prophecy is not such as would be congenial to the writer of the earlier part of 40–66. It is simpler then to regard it as referring to customs practised after the Return. In this case we can readily understand the conditions to which he refers. A certain number of Jews had been left behind in Judah after the captivities to Babylon and the flight of Johanan and many more into Egypt. This people of the land that was left probably belonged to the most superstitious stratum of Jewish society. It seems to have been further contaminated through connexion with the surrounding heathen population. Further, in Samaria the remnant of Israelites left after the downfall of the Northern Kingdom had been reinforced by heathen settlers. These facts amply explain the existence of gross heathen practices among the Israelitish and Jewish peoples in Palestine. It is also not unlikely that in 66[1] we have a reference, as Duhm has conjectured, to the Samaritan project of building a Temple. It is quite clear that the prophet, whether the Second Isaiah or a later writer, could not, in view of numerous passages to the contrary, be depreciating the Temple at Jerusalem. He might be attacking the unspiritual worshippers who wished to erect a Temple, assuring them that Yahweh desired no temple from such as they were. But this hardly agrees with the language used by the Second Isaiah, whether in 40–55 or in later chapters, in which much stress is laid on the Temple. The explanation which brings it into relation with the Samaritan Temple meets the conditions fairly well. It must be remembered that Haggai complains of the character of the people and yet urges them to rebuild the Temple. It is further significant that there is a great contrast between the tone of 40–55 and that of much of 56–66. This comes out in various ways. While in the former we have the prophet exulting in near deliverance, in the latter there are references to delay. In the 59th chapter the prophet complains that salvation is far from them (verses 9–11). He gives as the reason for this that the iniquities of the people have effected a separation between themselves and God. It is not that Yahweh's hand is so shortened that He cannot save, but that the people are themselves so steeped in sin. The glowing prophecy of the splendours of Zion in 60 ends with the words : ' I the Lord will hasten it in its time.' Again stress is laid much more than by the Second Isaiah on the externals of religion such as the Temple service and keeping of the Sabbath. The description of the social condition of the community agrees better with the view that it consisted no longer of exiles in Babylon, but of a people, who, without being politically independent, yet possessed a large degree of self-government. It is true that this is not decisive because we know so little of the circumstances of the exiles in Babylon. The general affinities are, however, with the state of things reflected in the post-exilic prophets, especially Malachi, and this applies not only to social but also to religious conditions, especially to the division into parties. And although there are close similarities in language and idea between 56–66 and 40–55, the difference in tone and point of view is very marked. The coincidence may readily be explained on the theory of imitation.

On the question whether 56–66 is itself composite, no more need be said than is said on pp. 70—1. Nor is it necessary to discuss the view that the work of the Second Isaiah ended with 48. The two sections 40–8 and 49–55 are bolted together by the Servant passages. On these see Appendix C.

The Servant of Yahweh

IT is unnecessary to linger over the passages in which the Servant of Yahweh is unquestionably Israel. But the four passages already mentioned (42^{1-4}, 49^{1-6}, 50^{4-9}, 52^{13}–53^{12}), which may for convenience be called the Servant passages, have for the last twelve years aroused keener discussion than perhaps any other Old Testament problem. The questions at issue are both critical and theological, and touch the authorship of the passages and their interpretation. The question of authorship is to some extent associated with that of interpretation. If the passages are the work of the Second Isaiah, there is a rather strong presumption that he means by the Servant in them what he has meant in other parts of the prophecy that is Israel. On the other hand, the converse of this proposition would not be so probable, for if it were to be determined that in these passages the Servant meant the same as in the rest of Isaiah 40–55, identity of authorship could not be inferred from this, inasmuch as two writers might speak of Israel as the Servant. Again, if difference of meaning could be established, identity of author would be improbable. But if difference of author were established, nothing more would follow than that one of the reasons for accepting identity of interpretation would disappear. Yet each of the four alternatives has its representatives. The usual view has been that we have identity of author and identity of meaning. Sellin, however, has argued for identity of author with difference of meaning. Wellhausen and Smend accept difference of authorship with identity of meaning. Duhm and several other scholars argue for difference of author and difference of meaning. It may be urged that since the Servant passages seem only loosely connected with their context, it is likely that they were not inserted here by the Second Isaiah himself. But it is still less likely that anyone else inserted them in an apparently quite unsuitable context, whereas there may have been subtle points of connexion in the author's mind, which do not at all lie on the surface. Some scholars have argued with considerable force that such points of contact may be discovered. We may also leave open the possibility that the Second Isaiah composed the Servant passages at an earlier period, and worked them into the main body of his prophecy, or even that he composed them later and inserted them, though this is improbable.

It is better to attack the problem on the exegetical than the critical side, and from an examination of the passages themselves discover the significance assigned in them to the figure of the Servant. The main question is whether the Servant is an individual or Israel. It will be convenient to discuss the individual interpretation first.

The credit of establishing, to the satisfaction of many recent scholars, that the Servant is to be regarded as an individual, belongs to Duhm. In his commentary on Isaiah published in 1892, he assigns the four Servant passages to the age of Nehemiah, and accounted for their present position by saying that they were inserted where there happened to be room in the margin or between sections of the prophecy, a wholly frivolous explanation. The Servant was a contemporary of the author of the poems. He was a teacher of the Law, and a leper, despised and persecuted by his countrymen. After his death from leprosy and burial in dishonour, his disciples, of whom the author was one, expected him to rise again and in his exaltation accomplish God's great purpose. Kittel and Sellin revived an earlier view that the Servant in Isaiah 52^{13}–53^{12} was Zerubbabel, who was supposed to have been put to death by the Persians for revolt in connexion with a Messianic movement. Sellin's view was combined with a very complicated literary theory as to the composition of the Second Isaiah. He has since withdrawn the identification with Zerubbabel, and now fixes on Jehoiachin as the Servant. Bertholet adopts a collective interpretation for the Servant passages in general, but regards nearly the whole of Isaiah 53 as an insertion, written on the fate of Eleazar, a martyr in the persecution of Antiochus Epiphanes. In the first edition of his *Alttestamentliche Religionsgeschichte*, Smend modified Duhm's view in two respects. He regarded the Martyr referred to as living and dying before the time of the Second Isaiah, who incorporated the Servant passages in his work, and he thought the Servant was not to be interpreted in the same way in all of them. He adopted the individual interpretation of 50^{4-9}, 52^{13}–53^{12}, but in 42^{1-4} and 49^{1-6} identified the Servant with Israel, since in the latter passage the Servant before his resurrection speaks as if he were still living, which does not suit the individual. He also interpreted the resurrection of the martyr as metaphorical, the Servant does not rise from the dead, but he lives again in the successors who carry on his work. In his second edition (1899) he has withdrawn this view and identifies the Servant in all four passages with Israel.

The strength of the individual interpretation lies in the fact that the language of some of the passages and especially of 52^{13}–53^{12} seems to point to some definite individual as in the prophet's mind. Probably some will always find it impossible to believe that this language can refer to anything but an individual. It is, however, exposed to very grave objections. In the first place we must reckon with the fact that the Servant passages are at present found in a prophecy in which the Servant of Yahweh is identified with Israel; there is therefore a presumption that in these passages this identification should be maintained. In the next place this identification is actually made in the present text of one of our Servant passages : ' Thou art My servant : Israel, in whom I will be glorified ' (49^3). Duhm has accordingly to strike out the word ' Israel ', but there is no real justification for this, apart from difficulties that may be felt in the national interpretation. Smend retained the word in his first edition, but, as already mentioned, while he held that in the first two Servant passages the Servant was Israel, he adopted an individual interpretation for the last two. This position, however, is very difficult; the same view should be taken in all four passages. A third difficulty is the idea, at this date, of a resurrection of the Servant, since elsewhere we find the thought of individual resurrection in much later passages. This difficulty is not insuperable. If the Servant was an individual, the impression he made was so great that a conviction that death could not hold him would not have been altogether unnatural. Fourthly, it is very hard to believe that an Old Testament prophet could have spoken of any contemporary in such language as we find in 52^{13}–53^{12}. This is not merely on account of the representation of the Servant as suffering vicariously for those who utter 53^{4-6}, but on account of the world-wide notice attracted by him and the world-wide influence that he exerts. He will startle many nations and kings shall be dumb with astonishment before him. So in 49^{1} the Servant bids the far lands and the nations listen, and in verse 6 says that Yahweh has given him for a light to the Gentiles, to be His salvation to the ends of the earth. In the first passage, 42^{1-4}, he is to bring forth judgement to the nations, he is to set judgement in the earth and the far lands wait for his teaching. It is highly improbable that the prophet should have formed so exalted a conception of any contemporary as to have believed that he would rise from his dishonoured grave and undertake so succesful a mission to the heathen world. And how are we to suppose that whole nations and their kings were startled by the transformation in the fortunes of a despised and persecuted leper, of whom during his lifetime they would never have heard ? There is nothing to show that the Servant was a king or prince, who might have attracted attention of this kind.

It seems, then, that the objections to an individual interpretation are very cogent. The question there-

fore arises whether in spite of the features which
seem so strongly to point to a person, we should
not accept the identification of the Servant in some
sense with Israel. This is supported by 49³ and the
LXX text of 42¹. It is held in various forms, the
Servant being regarded as the historical nation,
or the righteous kernel of the nation, or the prophetic
order, or the ideal Israel. The most obvious explanation is that the historical Israel is meant. The
word is thus used in its strict sense, as we have
a right to expect, unless we are warned to the contrary,
and the Servant thus bears the same significance here
as in the rest of 2 Isaiah. This view has been
defended above all by Giesebrecht, but also by Budde
and Marti, and is accepted among others by
Wellhausen, Smend, Cornill, Siegfried, and H. P.
Smith. In spite of this weighty array of supporters,
many scholars regard it as exposed to insuperable
objections. In the first place it is said that the
description given of the Servant does not correspond
to the actual character and career of Israel. The
Servant is an innocent sufferer, but the prophets
represent Israel as suffering for its own sin, and
the Second Isaiah himself does so. It is best to
consider this with a second objection. If Israel
suffers for the sins of others, these can only be the
heathen. Accordingly we must regard the heathen
as speaking in the former part of chapter 53, as
confessing their misconceptions of the Servant
and saying that he has suffered for their sins. It
is urged that this is incredible on the lips of the
heathen, and if the prophet had meant this he would
have said it explicitly. The former of these objections
is very precarious, the passage is of a very extra-

ordinary character in any case, and we cannot rule out an interpretation because it expresses something very surprising to us. As to the latter objection, we cannot demand that the prophet should introduce the speakers explicitly. The sudden burst into speech at the beginning of 53 is fine and effective, and similar cases occur elsewhere. Moreover, we must not judge what the prophet may have thought necessary for clearness by what his readers may feel to be necessary. If he identified the Servant with Israel in his own mind, then he would regard it as self-evident that the speakers in the former part of 53 must be the heathen nations. All we could reasonably expect would be that an intimation should be given in the context. And this we have in the immediately preceding verse (52[15]). The Servant is to startle many nations, and kings are to be dumb with amazement before him. It is therefore not far-fetched to suppose that after this we have an expression of their astonishment. This we get in 53[1] which may quite well be translated ' Who would have believed that which we have heard ? but to whom has Yahweh's working been revealed ? ' The meaning is that they have heard the wonderful news of the Servant's exaltation, and their first thought is : ' Who could ever have believed that this high destiny was reserved for him ? ' They then go on to excuse their blindness to his true character. He was like a dwarfed and sickly plant with no beauty or promise, like a leper cursed by God. Then they proceed to confess that the curse which they thought rested upon him, was really the punishment for their own sin. In this way we get a perfectly connected line of thought.

These deep truths are not strange on the lips of the nations, for it is not the nations in their heathen blindness who are speaking, but the nations who have witnessed the exaltation of the Servant and have come to recognize Yahweh as the true God. The train of thought which leads up to their conclusion is not hard to discover. They have seen Israel enduring unparalleled suffering, and have explained it to be due to its unparalleled sin. But now they find from Israel's exaltation that Israel has been righteous. How then account for its suffering? If it is not due to its own sin, then may it not be due to theirs? They have gone astray into idolatry, Israel has clung to the true God. But Israel has suffered, while they have gone free. What they have deserved Israel has endured. Its suffering has been vicarious. All this is a perfectly natural explanation of the passage. But if it is the heathen nations that speak in the former part of chapter 53, much of the first objection is removed. This was that the prophets, including the Second Isaiah, regarded Israel as guilty and suffering for its own sin, while the Servant is represented as innocent and suffering for the sins of others. But some of the strongest expressions of the latter thought occur in the former part of chapter 53. If this contains the confession of the heathen, it must be judged as spoken from their point of view. Naturally in their revulsion of feeling, in their recognition of their own sinfulness and the extreme suffering of Israel, they look on Israel as innocent in comparison with themselves, and therefore as suffering for the world's sin, not for its own. Still, this does not entirely remove the difficulty. The author of the Servant passages speaking in his own person, expresses similar ideas about the Servant. It may be he who speaks of him as righteous, says that he had done no violence, neither was deceit in his mouth. In 50[5] the Servant says : ' I was not rebellious, neither turned away backward.' Yet these expressions are quite compatible with a recognition of sin in the Servant ; freedom from violence and deceit is by no means the same thing as sinlessness. Moreover, the Second Isaiah's estimate of Israel was more favourable than that of the earlier prophets, though he does speak strongly of Israel's sin. It is also very important to observe that he considers Israel's punishment to have been excessive : ' She hath received at the Lord's hands double for all her sin.' If Israel has received double punishment, it is not far from this to the thought that the suffering it has not deserved has been for the sin of other nations. In comparison with these Israel might be regarded as righteous. It is not of an absolute but of a relative righteousness that the author is thinking. As confirming the interpretation that Israel suffers for the sin of the Gentile nations, it may be pointed out that in the first two servant passages the mission of the Servant to the Gentiles is emphasized, so that from the outset a close connexion is affirmed between the Servant and the Gentile world.

A third objection to the identification of the Servant with the historical Israel is that the two are expressly distinguished. This seems at first sight to be conclusive. In 53[8] the Servant seems to be regarded as smitten for the sin of Israel. But the text should be corrected and we should probably

read ' for our rebellions he was smitten to death '.
(See p. 50, note [b].)

The other passage which is thought to affirm a
distinction between Israel in the national sense
and the Servant is 49[5-6]. The usual view is that
here the Servant has, as part of his mission, the
function of restoring Israel from exile. There are
some general objections to this. Nowhere else is this
function assigned to the Servant, or mentioned in
the Servant passages. This is very remarkable,
whether we regard the passages as written by the
Second Isaiah or not. If they were written by
the Second Isaiah, it is very strange that he should
assign to the Servant what elsewhere he assigns
to Yahweh. It is also strange, considering that the
restoration of Israel is a main theme of his prophecy,
that it should here be introduced as affording
insufficient scope for the Servant's activity. But
it is strangest of all that the writer should speak
of the Servant as restoring Israel, when he has
frequently identified the Servant with Israel, and
has in fact just done so in this very passage. What
meaning are we to put on the statement that Israel
restores Israel from exile ? Similarly, if the Servant
passages are not by the Second Isaiah, this difficulty
still lies against the view that the Servant brings
back Israel from exile, unless in 49[3] we quite arbitrarily
delete ' Israel '. Besides, it would be very remarkable
that the author should assume, as if it were a well-
known function of the Servant, that he should
raise up the tribes of Jacob, although this is nowhere
else mentioned, and announce as a still further
achievement the mission to the Gentiles which
has already been emphasized in the first Servant

passage. Probably, however, the usual view of
49^{5-6} is incorrect (see p. 41, note [1],) and no
distinction between the Servant and Israel can be
based on this passage.

Fourthly, we have the fact, already mentioned,
that the language in some of the passages is so
personal in its character as to suggest very strongly
that an individual and not the nation is in the
prophet's mind. But we must not forget that
the personification of nations or other collective
bodies went very much farther in Hebrew than
would be permissible in English, and that this fact
is often disguised from English readers of the Bible,
since the expression has been toned down into
harmony with English idiom.[a] Thus in Joshua 9^7
the Revised Version translates : ' And the men
of Israel said unto the Hivites, Peradventure ye
dwell among us ', but the literal translation is :
' And the man of Israel said unto the Hivite, Peradventure thou art dwelling in my midst.' It is
generally admitted that in several of the Psalms
the first person singular stands for the nation,
though the range of this is greatly disputed. In
Lamentations also the nation speaks in the first
person singular. A very striking parallel to the
description of the Servant is found in Psalm 129^{1-3},
where we read : ' Many a time have they afflicted
me from my youth up,' and again : ' The plowers
plowed upon my back, they made long their furrows.'
These expressions in themselves suggest that an
individual sufferer is speaking, but the passage
definitely puts the words in Israel's mouth. We

[a] See a good note in Gray's *Numbers*, on ' The Personification
of Nations', pp. 265–6.

need not therefore feel obliged by the very marked character of the language to see in the Servant an individual. The nation is personified, though the personification is certainly remarkable.

The objections to the view that the Servant is the Israelitish nation, which has suffered death in the Exile and is to experience a glorious resurrection in the restoration, after which it will instruct the heathen in the true religion, seem therefore to be inconclusive. It has the great advantage that the Servant passages are thus brought into line with the general conception formed by the Second Isaiah of Israel's restoration and mission to the Gentiles. This relationship to the heathen along with the assertion that Israel has received a double punishment for her sin, supply the basis for the doctrine that Israel has suffered on account of the sins of the heathen. It is better to understand by the Servant the actual historical Israel than any section of Israel, such as the righteous kernel of the nation. The speakers in the former part of 53 would in that case be the rest of Israel. But as they had also suffered very heavily for their sin they would hardly be inclined to see in the spiritual Israel within Israel the vicarious sufferer for their sin. Nor do the individualizing features of the prophecy suit a number of persons in the nation so well as they suit the whole nation.

Nor need we with Cheyne, Skinner, and others interpret the Servant to be the ideal as distinguished from the historical Israel. There are certain advantages in this view. The language used is not too elevated, and there is not the difficulty that while Israel is regarded as sinful the Servant is righteous, since on this view the Servant is not the actual Israel. This interpretation helps to account for the features transferred to it from the history of Israel, or of the righteous remnant or even of such individuals as Jeremiah and the other prophets. These were so many realizations in fact of what existed in the ideal. But this view labours under serious difficulties. First there is the unquestionable fact that the Second Isaiah speaks of the Servant in language inapplicable to the ideal Israel. If then he is the author of the Servant passages, he uses the word in incompatible senses. Further, it is not quite natural for the Israelites to regard the ideal Israel as suffering for their sins. The thought might perhaps be of the persecutions endured by those in whom the ideal Israel had found its partial realization, true prophets and other pious Israelites. And where the more spiritual religion came in conflict with the traditional the adherents of the latter would regard the sufferings which the former entailed as manifest tokens of Divine displeasure, and thus we might say that the ideal Israel had to endure the misjudgement of the Israelites, who attributed its afflictions in its representatives to their adherence to what was false and sinful. Thus Jeremiah's doctrine of the overthrow of the nation and the destruction of the Temple contradicted an intense religious feeling that existed in the nation. This was a case in which the ideal Israel may be said to have come into collision with the actual and to have suffered at its hands. Yet while it is on these lines that an explanation would have to be sought, if there were no alternative to taking the Servant as the ideal Israel, the thought that the ideal Israel suffers for the sins of the Israelites is extremely artificial. Moreover, if we distinguish between the Servant and the actual Israel, it is not easy to avoid the conclusion that the Servant as a part of his mission has to restore Israel from Babylon. But what are we to make of the thought that the ideal Israel restores the actual Israel from exile? The best answer would perhaps be that the work assigned to Israel in the Divine plan, required its restoration, and since the actual was restored for the sake of the ideal, the work of restoration may be ascribed to the Servant. But there is plainly a difference between that for which a thing is done and that by which it is done, and the explanation reminds one too forcibly of some very risky New Testament exegesis. Lastly, we are under the disadvantage that we must omit the Exile from the sufferings of the Servant. By so doing we cut the passages away from the most important fact in the contemporary historical situation, and thus fail to find in them the author's solution of the problem that pressed most heavily on his contemporaries. This is all the more arbitrary, since the author has said at the outset that Jerusalem has suffered a double punishment for all her sin. This is explained, if part of the punishment has been vicarious. But if we identify the Servant with the ideal Israel we reach the strange result that while the actual Israel has received in the Exile twice as much punishment as it deserved, its sins are nevertheless atoned for by the sufferings of the ideal Israel, in which the Exile is not included. It is not probable that the Israelites who had suffered the penalty of exile would utter the thought that the ideal Israel had borne their sins.

For these reasons we must reject the identification of the Servant with the ideal Israel, and accept the view that the Servant is throughout the actual Israel, which died in the Exile and is to rise again in the Restoration. Nevertheless there is an element of truth which must be recognized in the view that the Servant is the ideal Israel. The nation is regarded in the light of its purpose in the mind of God. The Servant is not an ideal distinct from the nation, but the nation regarded from an ideal point of view. This accounts for all the phenomena, and introduces consistency into the representation more successfully than any of the rival interpretations, inasmuch as differences are due not to any change in the identity of the Servant, but simply to change in the aspect under which he is regarded.

Index